CONTENTS

Developed by the Editorial Team

TEACHING WITH LIMITED SPACE

"We don't have a classroom for our children—we have to meet in the sanctuary."

Could this be your comment? Here are some suggestions for the Sunday school with limited space and resources:

If your Sunday school class must meet in the sanctuary, your materials must all be portable. A corner of the sanctuary can be turned into a teaching area. Baskets or plastic storage bins can be used to hold supplies for different activities. Place the art supplies in one basket or bin. A plastic tablecloth on the floor can serve as a work surface for one or two children at a time. A laundry basket can hold blocks (wooden, cardboard, or covered milk cartons) for a building area.

A pew or a series of boxes could hold the Tinkertoy™ or Lego™ building blocks and accessories such as toy cars, trucks, and people. A bath mat or blanket will muffle the block noise if the floor is not carpeted.

Three cardboard boxes can be transformed into a family living center. One could be painted to look like a stove. Another could be cut to function as a tea table. The third box could become a doll bed or, if large enough, a house. Dress-up clothes, full-size plastic dishes, dolls, and doll clothes may be stored in the cardboard boxes.

Simple manipulative materials may be made and stored in shoeboxes. They may be used on a pew or on the floor and might include the following:

1) Spools and shoelaces for stringing.

2) A small board drilled with holes and a butter dish (with lid) filled with golf tees makes an inexpensive pegboard and pegs.

3) An egg carton and a box of large buttons can be used for sorting and counting.

4) Old teaching pictures can be mounted on cardboard or pressed wood, then cut into several pieces to make puzzles.

If your classroom space is even more cramped, consider moving the art projects to the hallway outside the classroom and moving out-of-doors for activities when weather permits.

Think Learning Centers. For a class of four to six children, two or three centers at a time might be sufficient. However, the centers that are available would need to be changed frequently. For instance, the Creative Art Center, Family Living Center, and Manipulatives could be available two consecutive Sundays. The next two Sundays the Creative Art Center, Building Center, and Family Living Center could be offered. Some things can be put away and other centers added during any one session.

Select those activities from the lesson plans that carry out the purposes of the unit. Provide for freedom of movement and creative expression. By adapting the available resources and space, the lesson plans can be tailor-made for your specific situation, and your children can have a sense of belonging to a community of faith where people care for and about people of every age.

By Jo Biggerstaff

Be an Invitational Teacher

INVITE CHILDREN INTO COMMUNITY

• by creating a welcoming and inclusive environment;
• by recognizing each child's gifts;
• by providing opportunities for children to develop self-esteem;
• by offering activities that foster cooperation rather than competition;
• by including many creative activities that encourage children to express their feelings;
• by providing opportunities for children to talk about their own ideas and experiences;
• by emphasizing their being a part of the larger body of Christ in the church;
• by encouraging teachers and classes to follow up on absent members.

INVITE CHILDREN INTO ACTION

• by using stories, activities, and projects that involve responding to the needs of others;
• by encouraging them to invite others to Sunday school and to share their faith in ways that are appropriate for their age level;
• by helping them learn to make choices and moral decisions based on Jesus' teachings.

INVITE CHILDREN INTO CONTINUING GROWTH

• by nurturing your own spiritual growth;
• by improving your teaching skills and by making the classtime inviting to children;
• by being loving, kind, and caring in your interaction with students to show them what Christians are like;
• by talking about your faith with your students and by helping them to talk about their own developing faith;
• by taking advantage of "teachable moments" as well as moments for meaningful worship.

INVITE CHILDREN INTO RELATIONSHIP WITH JESUS CHRIST

• by including times for worship and prayer;
• by increasing their familiarity with the Bible;
• by providing opportunities to learn and sometimes memorize Bible verses that tell about God's love and care;
• by using language that is appropriate for the age level when talking about religious or theological concepts;
• by helping them see how biblical concepts are related to experiences in their own lives;
• by inviting them to accept Christ as friend, teacher, Lord, and savior;
• by encouraging them to make commitments to follow Christ.

---

by Crystal A. Zinkiewicz and Linda R. Whited

Resources

The Bible

The New Revised Standard Version of the Bible is the primary Scripture resource for ONE ROOM SUNDAY SCHOOL.

One Room Sunday School Resource Kit

- Includes all four components—everything you need for a quarter.

Reproducible Activities Book

- Seven reproducible sheets for each week, including a Bible story and activities for a variety of age levels.

Teacher Book

- EasyTEACH® lesson plans for working with children of many ages in a single classroom. Includes teacher helps, lesson planning guides, and spiritual enrichment for the teachers.

Class Pak

- Thirty-two pages of large colorful teaching pictures, games, maps, posters, storytelling figures, songs, and more.

Compact Disc

- A forty-minute compact disc with music and stories for classroom use and teaching helps.

How to Use This Book

ONE ROOM SUNDAY SCHOOL resources are designed for classes where children of all ages learn together. The Teacher book includes suggestions for both group activities and individual activities. Some activities use reproducible activity sheets from this book. They are available for four groupings:

- For Nonreaders
- For Beginning Readers
- For Skilled Readers
- For Everyone

This symbol lets you know which groups in your class this sheet is designed for.

NR = Nonreaders
BR = Beginning Readers
SR = Skilled Readers

Choose the activities that will work best in your class. Then simply tear out those sheets on the perforated edge and photocopy the appropriate sheets for each child.

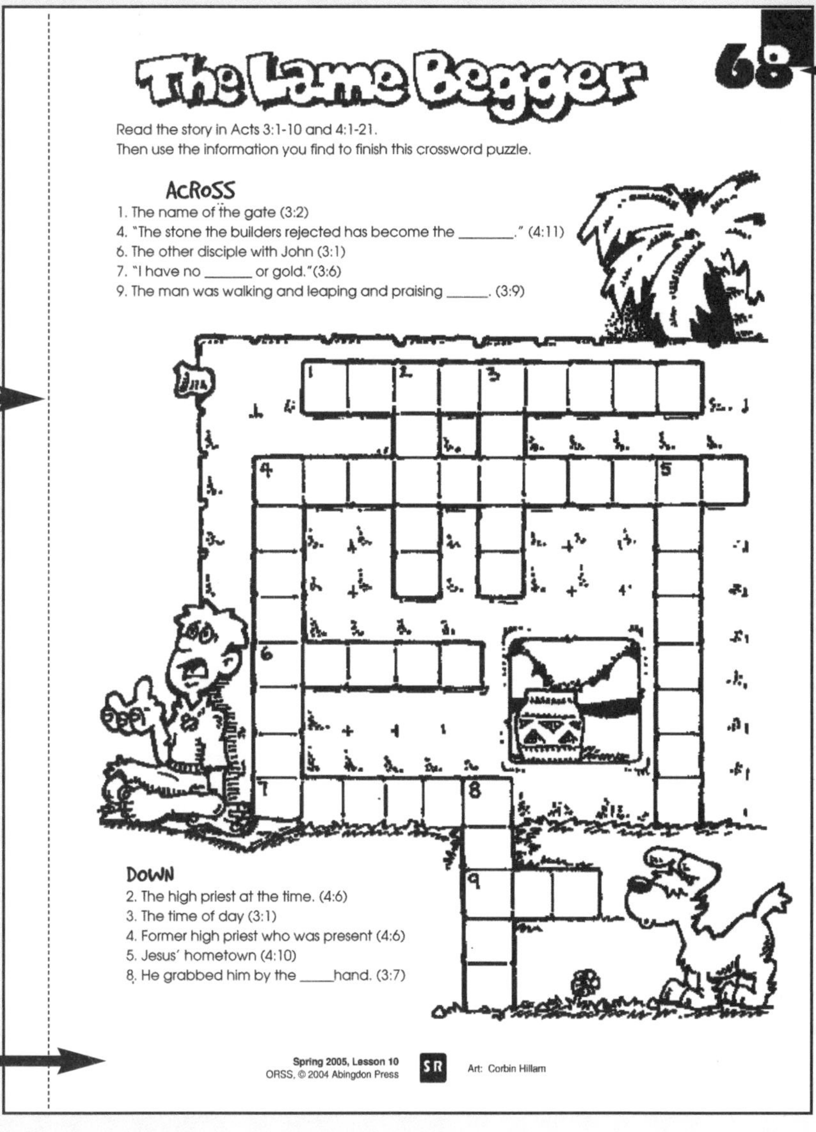

The Lame Begger

68

Each activity sheet clearly numbered for easy identification

Read the story in Acts 3:1-10 and 4:1-21.
Then use the information you find to finish this crossword puzzle.

ACROSS
1. The name of the gate (3:2)
4. "The stone the builders rejected has become the _______." (4:11)
6. The other disciple with John (3:1)
7. "I have no ______ or gold."(3:6)
9. The man was walking and leaping and praising ______. (3:9)

Perforated edge to make it easy to remove the page for photocopying

DOWN
2. The high priest at the time. (4:6)
3. The time of day (3:1)
4. Former high priest who was present (4:6)
5. Jesus' hometown (4:10)
8. He grabbed him by the _____hand. (3:7)

Groupings and lesson numbers at the bottom of each sheet

Spring 2005, Lesson 10
ORSS, © 2004 Abingdon Press
SR
Art: Corbin Hillam

on the Road Again

In the book of Mark we read about the many places Jesus went.

Mark 1:9; Mark 1:16; Mark 1:21; Mark 10:46; Mark 11:1-2; Mark 10:46-47; Mark 11:8-10

Look up each of these verses. Locate the city or place on the map and draw a line from the picture to the correct place on the map.

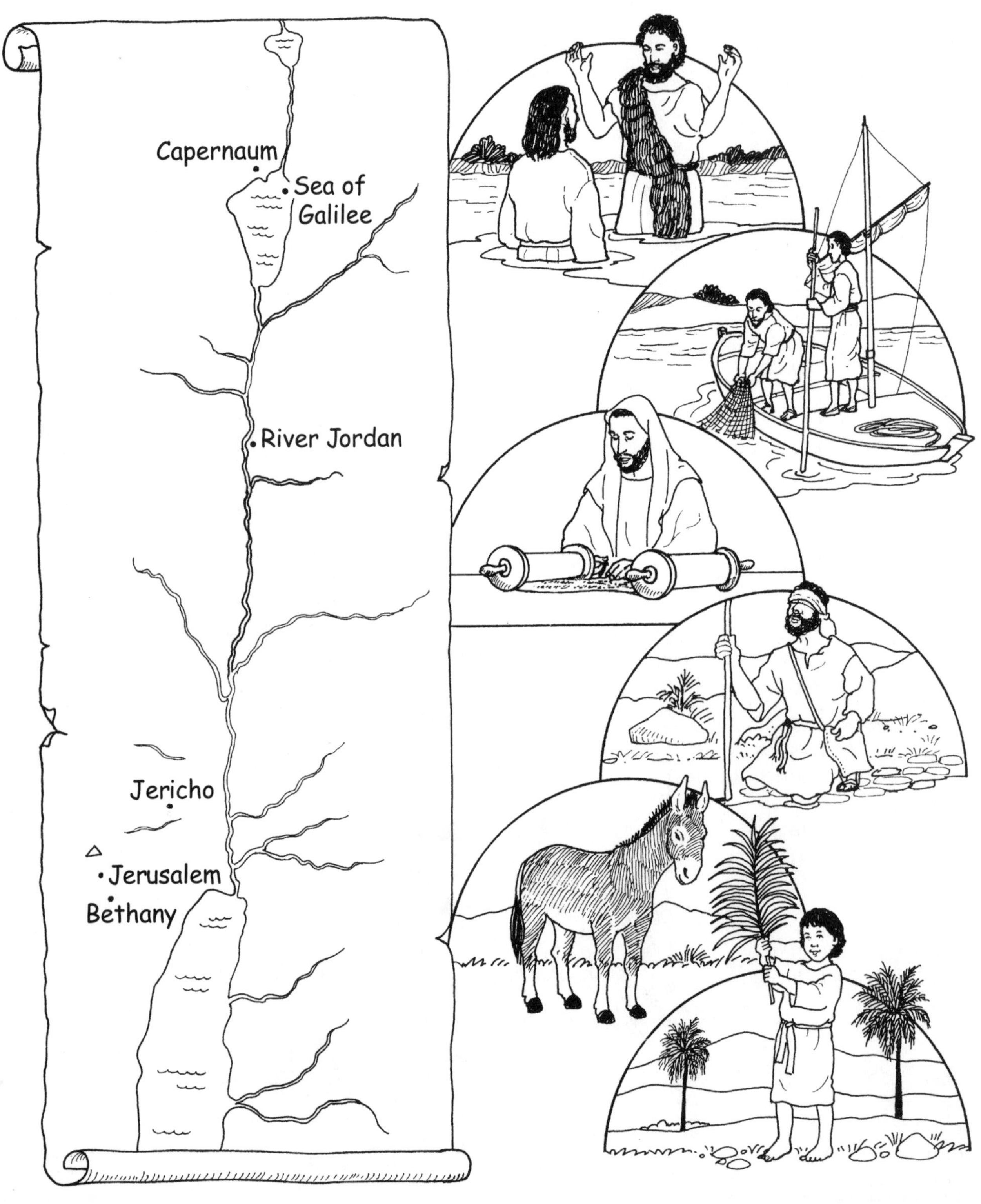

BR SR
Art: Yoshi Miyake

Save Us Now!

GROUP 1: We've left our home and left our fields. We're going to Jerusalem to celebrate Passover.

GROUP 2: Singing, laughing, as we go. Tell the stories of our people celebrating freedom.

CROWD: We need a Savior, one to save us. Send a Savior, send one now!

GROUP 1: At Passover we remember. We remember that we were once slaves in Egypt.

GROUP 2: We tell the story of how God sent Moses to save us. At Passover we will thank God.

CROWD: We need a Savior, one to save us. Send a Savior, send one now!

GROUP 1: But it is hard to think of freedom when everywhere you look there are Roman soldiers.

GROUP 2: We are not free as long as the Romans tell us what to do.

CROWD: We need a Savior, one to save us. Send a Savior, send one now.

GROUP 1: But Jesus walks among us. We've seen him with his friends. He'll bring us peace.

GROUP 2: Jesus is the Savior. He's the one who'll save us. He'll bring us peace.

CROWD: We need a Savior, one to save us. Send a Savior, send one now!

GROUP 1: He's riding on a donkey, one he borrowed just for this.

GROUP 2: The prophets told us our Savior would come riding on a donkey.

CROWD: We need a Savior, one to save us. Send a Savior, send one now!

GROUP 1: Hosanna! Our Savior is coming. Throw your coats down on the road.

GROUP 2: Hosanna! Our Savior is coming. Wave your palm branches as he passes.

CROWD: We need a Savior, one to save us. Send a Savior, send one now!

GROUP 1: Jesus is here! Jesus will save us! Jesus will bring us peace.

GROUP 2: Jesus will free us from the Romans! Jesus will bring us peace.

CROWD: We need a Savior, one to save us. Send a Savior, send one now!

GROUP 1: Hosanna! Blessed is the one!

GROUP 2: He comes in the name of the Lord.

CROWD: We need a Savior, one to save us. Send a Savior, send one now!

(Based on Mark 11:1-11)
Story by Linda Crooks

3

Color the Picture

NR

Art: Karol Kaminski

MAKE A DONKEY

1. Cut a one-inch slit in one end of a toilet paper tube. Cut a smaller slit in the other end across from the large slit.

2. Turn the tube over. Punch two holes near the front of the tube and the back of the tube to provide a place for the donkey's legs.

3. At both ends, run a pipe cleaner up into the tube through one hole and back down through the second hole. Pull until the ends of the pipe cleaner are even. Then twist the pipe cleaner tightly against the tube to create two legs. Twist and bend the pipe cleaners until the legs look realistic and the tube stands firmly on all four "feet."

4. Color the heads and the tails brown or gray.

5. Cut out the heads and the tails, leaving them joined. Fold each piece on the dotted line.

6. Glue the two head pieces together except for the ears.

7. Insert the head into the long slit on the toilet paper tube. Fold the two ears so that they stand out from the head.

8. Glue the tail together. Insert it into the smaller slot on the tube.

9. Draw a black cross on the donkey's back.

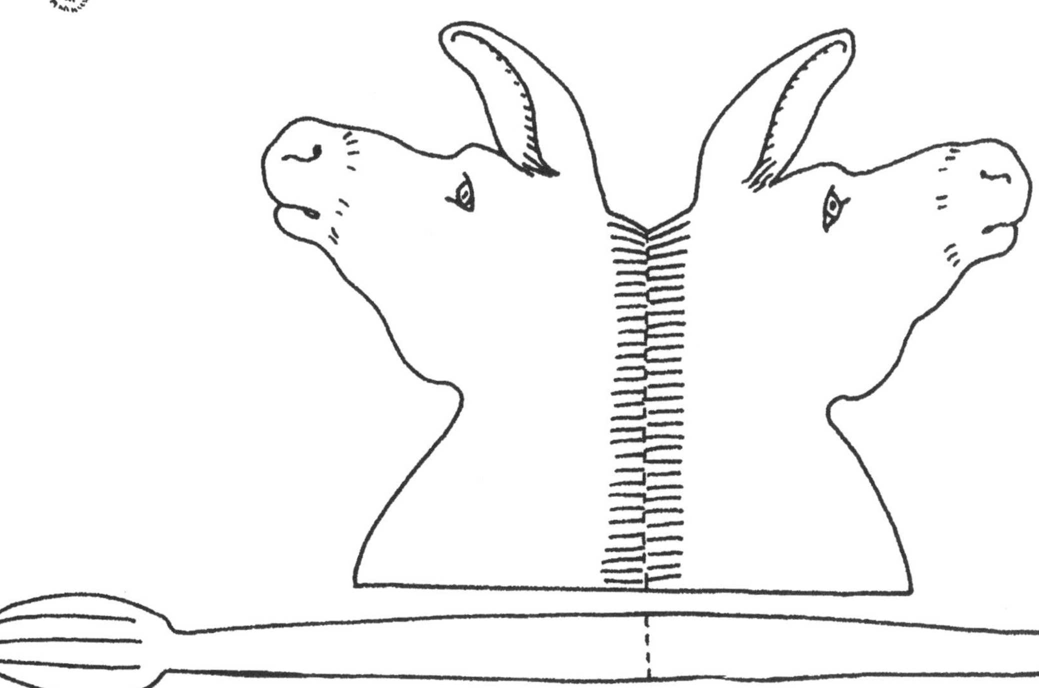

Art: Barbara Upchurch

Make a welcome poster for Jesus!

Decorate each letter. Then cut out the letters and glue them onto a piece of construction paper to create an interesting design.

Write:

<u>**Blessed is the one who comes in the name of the LORD! (Mark 11:9b)**</u>

on your poster.

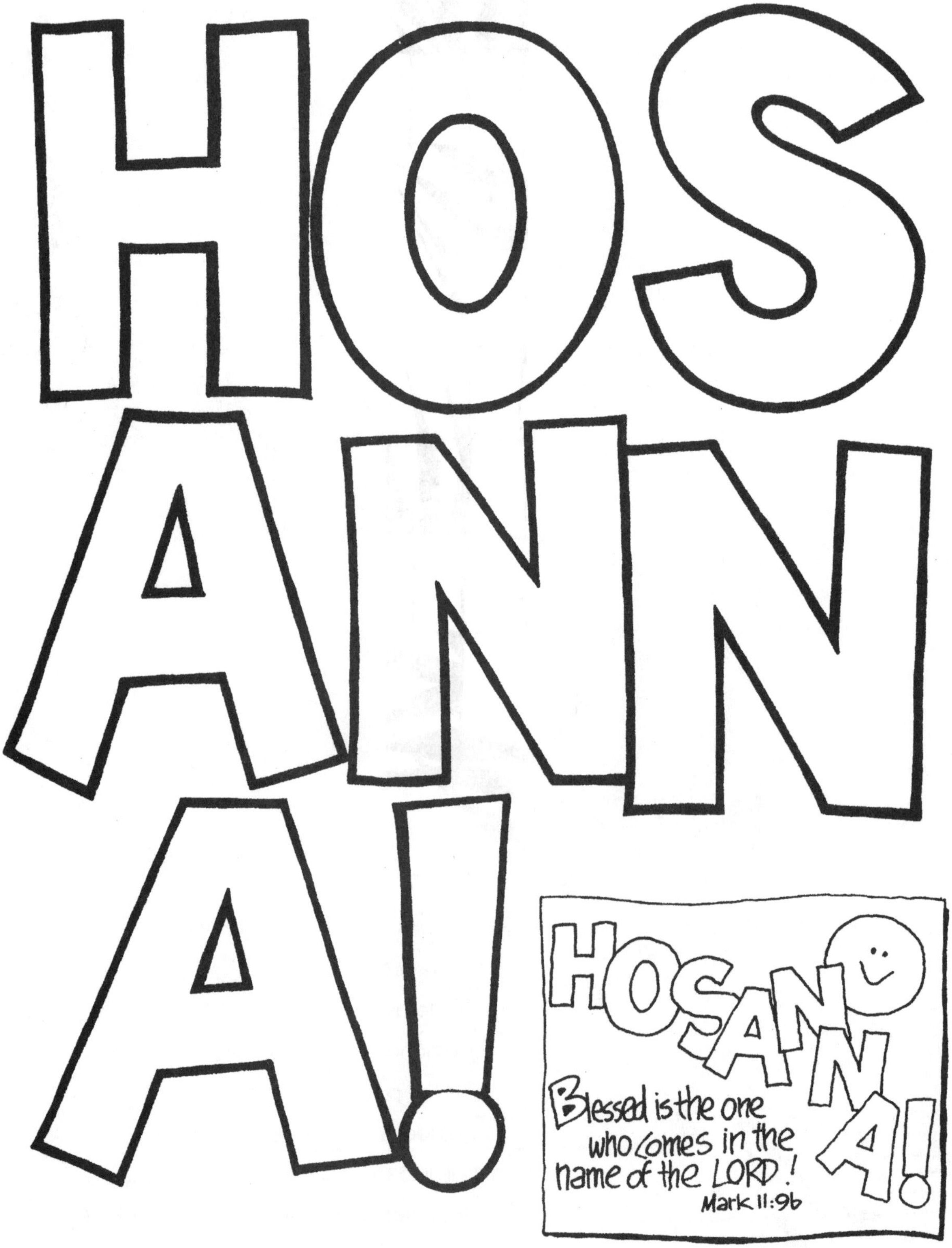

HOS
ANN
A!

HOSANNA!
Blessed is the one who comes in the name of the LORD!
Mark 11:9b

Art: Bob Jones

BIBLE CROSSWORD

1 2 3 4 5 6 8 9

What city was Jesus preparing to enter? (1 DOWN)

Who did Jesus send ahead of time? (8 ACROSS)

What did Jesus tell them they would find? (5 DOWN)

Who questioned what they were doing? (4 ACROSS)

What did the people shout when they saw Jesus? (9 ACROSS)

Jesus was identified as whose descendant? (6 DOWN)

What building did Jesus enter? (3 ACROSS)

When Jesus left the city, where did he go? (2 DOWN)

SR

Art: Brenda Gilliam

Advanced King Word Search

Look up these Bible verses. In each verse you will find one or more words that refer to a king—specifically in most verses to the kingship of God and Jesus. Find the words in the puzzle and explain to a friend what each one tells us about Jesus.

You should find 12 words.

MAJESTY Hebrews 1:3b
RICH 2 Corinthians 8:9
ROYAL James 2:8
THRONE, KINGDOM *(2 words)* Psalm 103:19
ALMIGHTY Genesis 17:1
CROWN Matthew 27:29
MAJESTY Exodus 15:7
AUTHORITY Matthew 9:6
DOMINION, RULES *(2 words)* Psalm 22:28a
SPLENDOR 1 Chronicles 16:29b

S E R K P O W L F K V Y B I L J A X S E L A Y O R
P T I H E T Q H Y W O I T M V U B I C L I T U K D
L O A G U S E I P G S P U R O P L E N D E Q E Z O
E N U L I M O Y E B E K R J I H R Y W P T Q N W H
N S T Y M K T S L 8 R R A A H T O M D E P S R E S
M O D O M I N I O N I P L H E C N K A Y R O K C D
A Y R E H V G J W J N C J 2 S R I C T Y O V E U O
L P V X O G L H Y C G I R O W E O Y H L M E D H N
R O Y O S 7 E M T U U R V N U T N E E J C R Z A A
P W D M X W V O P Y H Y Y J A M C R O W N E W R S
S E A B H C L 6 W N L V K E U P R U M D S I M E Q
B R S I P O C L M T V E Y S D O N L T M Y G C Q R
H F Y J A U R I T Y A R I T D T R E F O C N A H E
W U E O M B G I C H X Y L N E U Y S U L R N D 3 D
Y L O S Y T A S T Y A T E J R G S A L D B O 5 E S
L A M Y I C L K H I J L N K E D O M I N K D K C B
J S H I G N U I Y T P W T I V H V A D L D A I D A
U Y M Q H D E N S S H E K N S D G J T X I C N C E
S W W A T R G A L M O D A G I P N O I O J S D Z L
A S G K Y M M A J E S T Y D R W D U 4 V D D M E A
K I Q I O T I K G M D N A O D N T H G T H Y J D A
J N O C S Y L C P Q E T L M S I M E Z Y G X E Y R
A O N G D I M R T O H I G W Y R R I C H B A C E G
T Z E W K K O 9 O Z V S T I R O I V G V L I A L W
G U C S P L E N D O R E R M Y J H O U S E U N P E
A E R D R K T M K U 9 I R X O X E Y G T J H G I S
S P M A W O B N I B T Y O J H S P O W D T E D C A
R T H R O N E H M O W H G U N B H G U M N W M T M
C R O S A L Y N K R P U J M A U T H O R I T Y I U

Art: John Jordan

A Disciple Remembers

It was a special time, the first day of Passover. Jews were in Jerusalem from everywhere to celebrate together.

We disciples had come with Jesus to eat the Passover meal and to remember that God had delivered our ancestors from slavery in Egypt. It was a thankful time.

We couldn't help wondering if God would deliver us from trouble. The chief priests and scribes wanted to kill Jesus because they were afraid of what he taught. It was a dangerous time.

But Jesus didn't seem concerned. He was thinking about finding a place for us to eat our Passover meal. He told some of us to go into the city. "You will see a man carrying a jar of water," he said. "He will have a room we can use for our supper. You will also find a young donkey and the owner will loan it to you so that I may ride into town. Go and make everything ready." It was a preparing time.

Later when we went to the upper room to eat the Passover meal, Jesus himself washed the dust from our feet as if he were a servant rather than our leader. Afterwards we ate roasted lamb, unleavened bread, and bitter herbs to remind us that God had delivered our people from slavery in Egypt. It was a remembering time.

Jesus told us that he wanted to share this meal with us before he suffered. We didn't know what Jesus meant. But Jesus took a cup of wine and gave thanks to God. Then he said, "Share this with one another, for I will not drink of it again until the kingdom of God comes." We looked at one another. It was a confusing time.

Next, Jesus took a loaf of bread and blessed it. He broke it into pieces and passed it for us to eat. "This is my body, which is given for you," he said. Puzzled we looked at one another; but inside, somehow, we knew, it was a loving time.

As we looked to him for understanding, Jesus continued, "Do this in remembrance of me." Somehow we knew that no matter what happened, Jesus did not want us to forget him. Jesus had given us a way to remember him. Each time we drink from the cup or break bread together, we remember Jesus' love for us. It is a special time for remembering.

And Jesus told us that one reason he would not be eating with us again was because one of us would betray him. We couldn't believe it. We were his special friends. He had taught us, and we went with him everywhere. How could one of us betray him? When we left the upper room that night, we left in confusion.

Adapted from a story by Julia Kuhn Wallace.

Passover Background

God commanded that Passover be observed. It is a celebration to remember how God delivered God's people out of slavery in Egypt. God sent many plagues to Egypt, trying to convince the Pharaoh to let the enslaved Hebrew people go free. Finally, one night God sent the worst plague yet. The word *Passover* comes from this final plague.

On this night, God promised to visit every home in Egypt. Unless that home had marked the door of the house with the blood of a perfect lamb, the firstborn son would die. If the door was marked, God would "pass over" that house, and no one inside that home would die. This plague finally convinced Pharaoh to let the people go.

During the Passover meal in a Jewish household, there are many symbolic things to remind the family of the first Passover. The father or grandfather leads the meal and the ceremony. The Seder (SAY der), or Passover meal, consists of: matzo, a bread made without yeast, which is a reminder of how quickly the Hebrews left Egypt (they could not wait for bread to rise); bitter herbs, such as horseradish, as a reminder of the bitterness of slavery; haroset, a mixture of nuts, apples, and wine—the sweetness is a reminder of the sweetness of hope—and this also looks like the mortar the Jews in Egypt used to make bricks all day in the hot sun.

The family dips parsley twice into salt water. The green reminds them of spring and hope. As they taste the salt, they remember the salty tears of the slaves.

The family also reclines on soft cushions, because now they are free people and may rest when they please. A roasted lamb shank bone is a symbol of the lamb the Israelites roasted and ate quickly on the night they left Egypt and a roasted egg is a symbol of new life.

This is the celebration Jesus and his disciples were sharing during the Last Supper. They were remembering how God had freed his people from slavery in Egypt.

When we, as Christians, celebrate Holy Communion (with bread and grape juice), we are remembering Jesus. Jesus instructs his followers to remember him this way.

Art: Charles Jakubowski

Glad Times/Sad Times

Jesus ate the Passover meal with his disciples in Jerusalem. Everyone was eating and having a good time. (SMILE)

But then Jesus told the disciples something that they did not understand, "In a little while, you will not see me anymore." (FROWN)

"But then in a little while, you will see me again." (SMILE)

The disciples didn't understand what Jesus meant. (FROWN)

Jesus told them, "I am telling you that you will cry and be sad, (FROWN)

but then soon you will be happy again. (SMILE)

It will be a kind of happiness no one can take away from you. (SMILE)

It is true that soon you will not see me. (FROWN)

But God will send the Holy Spirit to help you, and you will not be alone." (SMILE)

Based on John 14:26; 16:16-22

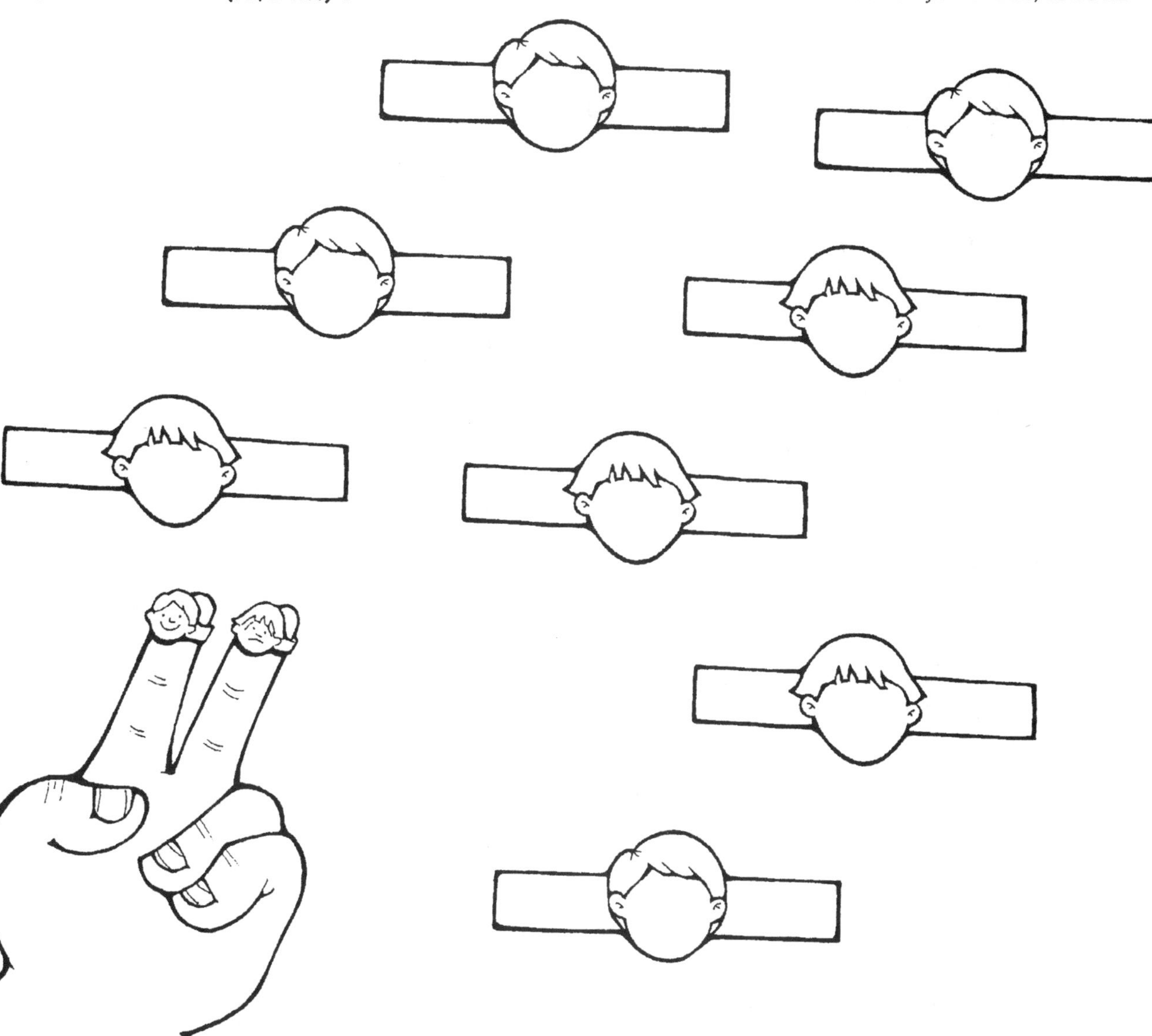

NR BR

Art: Megan Jeffery

11 Choose which items belong in Holy Communion.

NR BR

Art: Megan Jeffery

Butterfly Craft

SUPPLIES:
drawing paper; card stock cut into small, irregular pieces (old greeting cards, 3 x 5 cards, or posterboard); crayons; glue; scissors

1. Fold the drawing paper in half and then open it.

2. Glue the pieces of card close together on one half of the paper.

3. Fold the paper again and color over the top with one or more crayons.

4. Open the paper and cut the colored part off.

5. Fold the colored paper in half.

6. Draw half of a butterfly on the crease, cut it out and open it up.

7. Draw and cut out a body and antennae and glue them onto the butterfly.

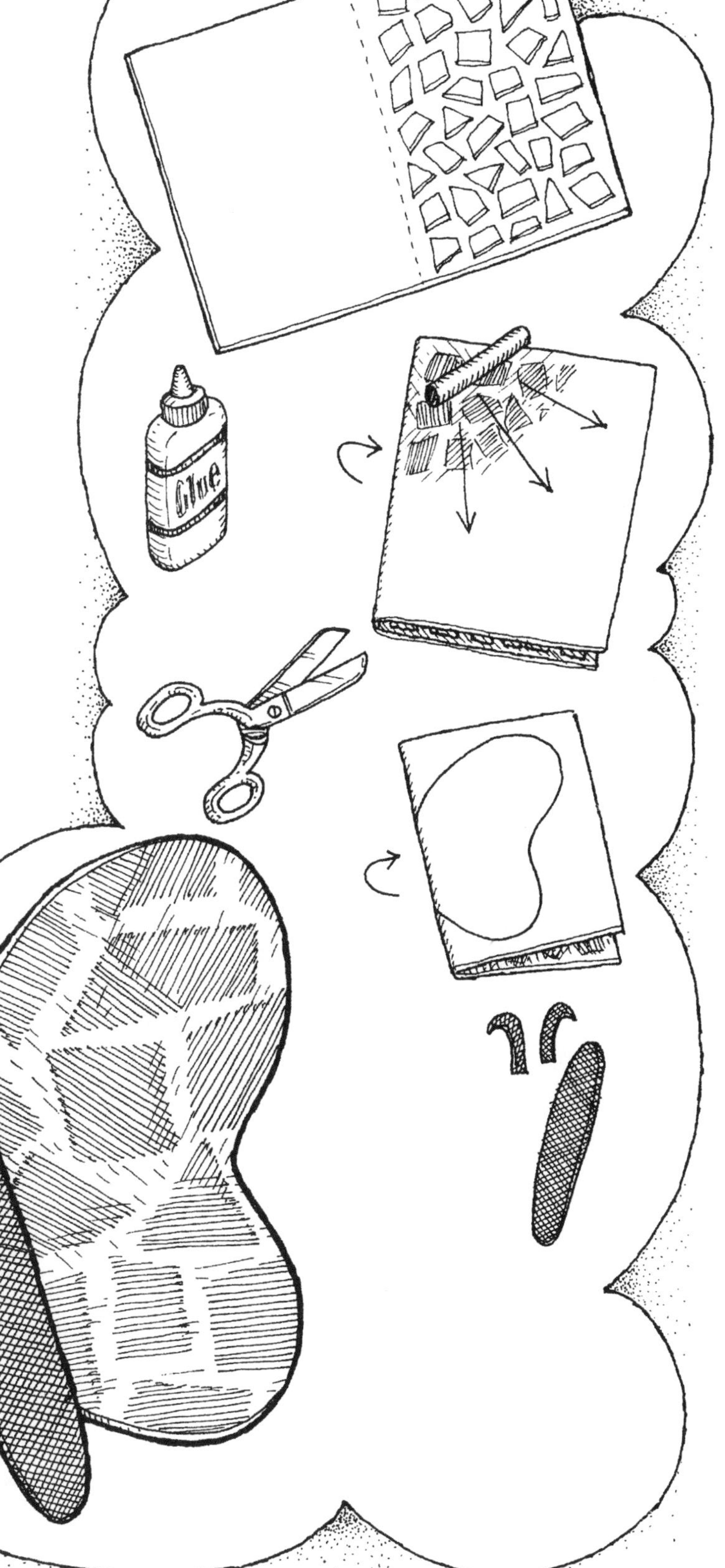

Art: Barbara Upchurch

13

Passover and Holy Communion

Passover is the beginning of the Jewish Festival of Unleavened Bread. What event do those who celebrate Passover celebrate and remember? (Exodus 12:39; 13:3)

When we celebrate **Holy Communion** in our churches today, what event do we remember? (Luke 22:15-19)

When is Passover celebrated? (Leviticus 23:5-6; Exodus 12:1, 2; 13:3-4)

When is Holy Communion celebrated? (Check with your teacher or pastor if you do not know the regular times for Holy Communion in your own congregation.)

What are the traditional foods that the Bible tells us were eaten at the Passover meal? (Exodus 12:8)

What is served at the Holy Communion meal to remind us of Jesus? (1 Corinthians 11:23-26)

Who is usually present for the Passover meal? (Exodus 12:3-4)

Who is usually present for the Holy Communion meal? (Think about when you receive Holy Communion.)

Art: Charles Jakubowski

JESUS AND HIS DISCIPLES

A Word to Learn: BETRAY

Betray means to be disloyal or to hand someone over to the hands of an enemy. One of Jesus' disciples betrayed Jesus to the hands of the chief priests.

BETRAYED BY A FRIEND

Jesus chose twelve men to be his special helpers. These men went with Jesus everywhere. Jesus taught them and Jesus trusted them. They were his friends, but one of them ***betrayed*** Jesus. Who was it?

____

Write down all the names of Jesus' disciples.
If you need help, you will find them listed in Mark 3:16-19.

____

____

____

____

____

____

____

____

____

____

____

____

Art: Brenda Gilliam

15

In the Garden

READER 1: Jesus knew what was about to happen. He really didn't want to die.

GROUP: Not what I want, but what God wants.

READER 2: So with his friends: Peter, James, and John, Jesus went to the garden to pray.

GROUP: Not what I want, but what God wants.

READER 3: Jesus knew that there was danger that night. He asked his friends to keep watch.

GROUP: Not what I want, but what God wants.

READER 4: When Jesus was apart from his friends, he threw himself down on the ground.

GROUP: Not what I want, but what God wants.

READER 5: God, I am sad. I am frightened. You, who can do anything, can make this go away. But not what I want, but what you want.

GROUP: Not what I want, but what God wants.

READER 6: Jesus got up and went to find his friends. They were sound asleep.

GROUP: Not what I want, but what God wants.

READER 1: Jesus scolded them, "Can't you stay awake for even one hour?"

GROUP: Not what I want, but what God wants.

READER 2: Jesus returned to the garden and prayed. "I don't want to do this. But it is not what I want, but what you want."

GROUP: Not what I want, but what God wants.

READER 3: And when Jesus returned to find his friends sleeping again, he said, "We don't have time for taking a rest. The time is here!"

GROUP: Not what I want, but what God wants.

READER 4: Judas led the soldiers into the garden. He went up to Jesus and kissed him.

GROUP: Not what I want, but what God wants.

READER 5: The soldiers fell upon Jesus. One of Jesus' friends drew his sword and attacked one of the soldiers, cutting off his ear.

GROUP: Not what I want, but what God wants.

READER 6: Jesus touched the soldier and healed him. Then he turned to the others and asked them, "Why do you come here at night with swords and clubs as though I were a thief? Every day I have been in the Temple teaching."

GROUP: Not what I want, but what God wants.

READER 1: And all of his friends ran away, leaving Jesus to the soldiers.

Based on Mark 14:32-51

Prayer Book

STAPLE

1

A Morning Prayer

Good morning, God,

Thank you for the rest I got during the night.

Be with me through the day.

Help me find ways to share your love with other people. Amen.

STAPLE

2

Prayer Before a Meal

O Great Creator,

Thank you for providing food for our table. As we eat, help us remember those who grew, harvested, and prepared this food. Bless those people who do not have enough to eat, and show us ways to help them. Amen.

STAPLE

3

A Prayer for Obedience

Dear God,
Please help me be good,
As I know I should.

When it's hard to obey,
Please show me the way.

Amen.

STAPLE

4

A Prayer for Those I Love

Loving God,

Bless my family and friends. Help us be kind and caring to each other.

Thank you for sending your Son to teach us how to be more loving. Amen.

Prayer Book

STAPLE

A Prayer for When I'm Scared or Sad

(sung to tune of "Twinkle, Twinkle, Little Star")

When I'm scared
Or when I'm blue
I know I can talk to you.
Give me peace
And make me calm.
Please be with me all day long.
When I'm scared
Or when I'm blue
I know I can talk to you.

STAPLE

Finger Prayer

Thumb: When I put a clenched hand to my chest, my thumb is the closest to my heart, so I remember to pray for my family and friends.

Pointer Finger: I pray for those who point me to the truth.

Middle Finger: My middle finger is my tallest finger, so I pray for leaders.

Ring Finger: The ring finger is the weakest finger. I pray for those who are weak or sick.

Pinky: My pinky is the smallest finger. I pray for people who cannot help themselves (such as people who are affected by war).

STAPLE

The ABC Prayer

This prayer helps us remember to include the following things as we pray:

A = Adoration—praise to God

B = Blessings for those I know and for me

C = Confession—admitting to God the wrong things I have done

D = Desires of my heart—I tell God what I really, really want.

E = Everyone—I pray that everyone will come to know Jesus.

STAPLE

A Nighttime Prayer

O God of Rest,

Thank you for the day that is ending.

Thank you for tomorrow and all the days to come.

Help me to rest peacefully, knowing that you are always near.

Amen.

Color the picture

Art: Benton Mahan

Circle the items of the words printed in bold print and discover how disciples share!

THOSE WHO SHARED

NARRATOR: Quick! Come with me to a gathering of Christians and listen. They do the most amazing things for one another.

MAN: Welcome to our meeting. Come, let me give you my **chair** to sit in.

WOMAN: My child had outgrown his **robe.** Is there someone here who has need of clothes?

BOY: I have something to share. My dog had **puppies.** Would anyone like one to play with?

TENTMAKER: I have just mended some **tents.** Is there anyone who needs shelter?

FISHERMAN: The catch last night was good. I have **fish** to offer. Is there anyone here who is hungry?

DISCIPLE: Thank you for sharing what you have.

BARNABAS: Wait, I have something to share too. I have just returned from Cyprus and have sold some land. Here is the **money** I received. I want to give this money to the poor.

DISCIPLE: Because we all share what we have with one another, we all have what we need. Thank God for each of you.

Based on Acts 2:44-45; 4:34-37

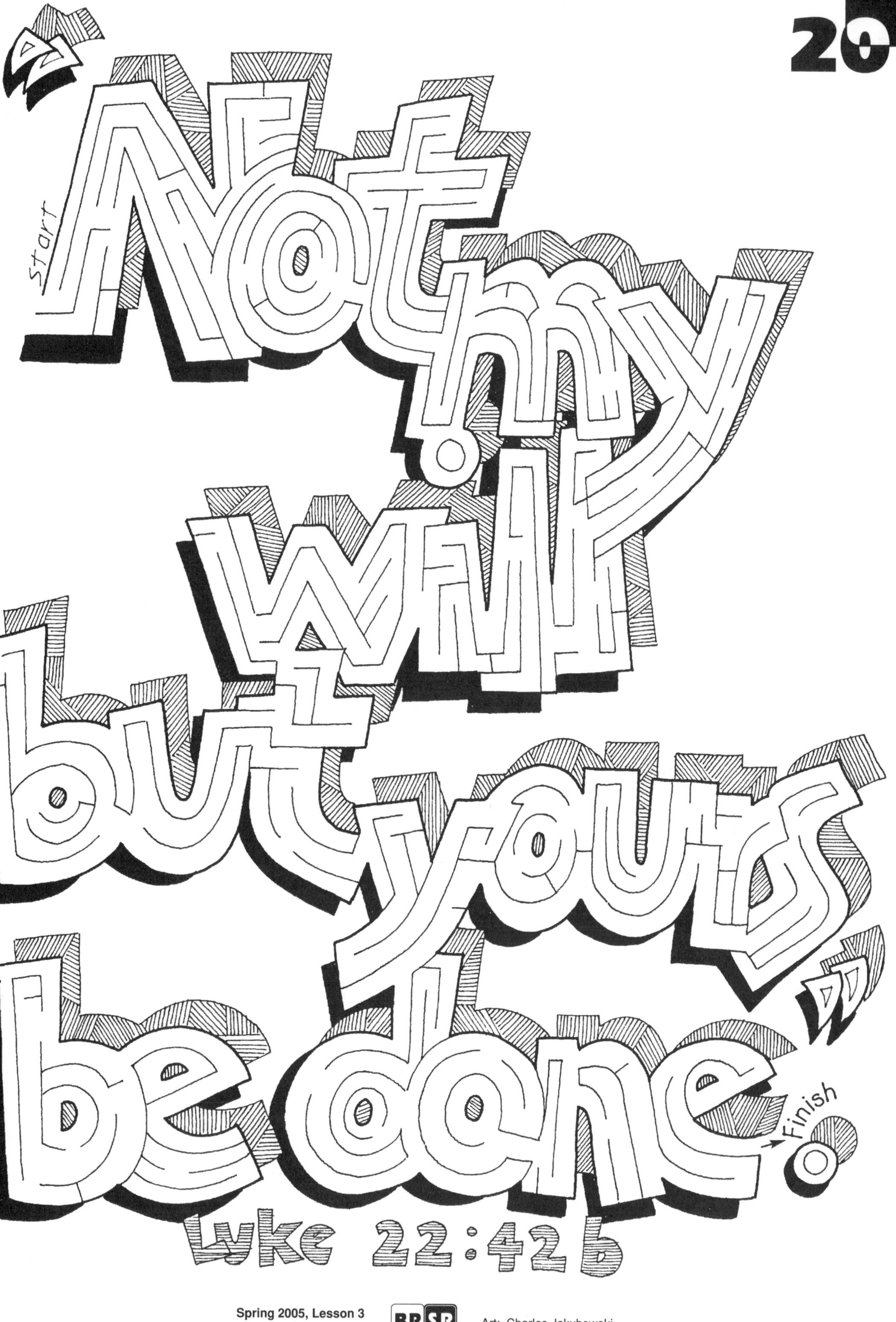

"Not my will but yours be done."

Luke 22:42b

start

finish

Art: Charles Jakubowski

Find the correct letter

for each blank to discover the answer Jesus received to his prayer. Use these clues:

C=A J=H G=E P=N.

Then see if you can guess the remaining letters based on the letters that you have filled in.

C P

C P I G N

C R R G C T G F

V Q

J K O

C P F

I C X G

J K O

U V T G P I V J

Check your answer by reading Luke 22:43

SR Art: Jim Padgett

A Most Wonderful Day

Two women made their way through the city streets on the day of the sabbath, just before the sun rose above the hills. Mary and Mary Magdalene were walking toward the tomb in the garden. They were going to attend to the body of their friend Jesus.

As they walked the two women wondered what they would do when they got to the tomb where Jesus was buried. A great stone had been placed across the tomb entrance. The stone was much too heavy for either of the two women to move.

The earth began to shake and tremble as the two women went near the garden. They looked at one another in fear. What could be happening?

The earthquake was caused by an angel of the Lord coming down from heaven into the garden. The angel went to the tomb and rolled back the heavy stone. Then the angel sat on the stone and waited for the two women to come into the garden.

When they saw the angel, Mary and Mary Magdalene were afraid. They had never seen such a being. The angel was as bright as lightening and his clothing was as white as snow. The guards that had been standing near the stone at the entrance to the tomb were now lying on the ground in the garden. The two women wondered if the guards were dead since they were so still. But the guards were only unconscious. The garden was very still.

Then the angel spoke. "Don't be afraid," he said. "I know you are looking for Jesus who was crucified. But he is not here. God has raised Jesus from the dead. Look into the tomb and see for yourself."

The two women walked past the heavy stone and peered into the tomb. In the spot where Jesus had been lying there were just the burial cloths. Jesus was not there.

"See," said the angel. "Now, go quickly and tell the others. Tell them that they are to meet Jesus in Galilee. This is my message to you."

So the two women quickly left the garden to find the other disciples. They wanted to share the good news with all their friends. Jesus was alive! As they left the garden, the two women met Jesus.

"Greetings," Jesus said to the two women. "Don't be afraid. Go and tell my brothers to go to Galilee. There they will see me."

What a wonderful day it was!

Jesus is alive!

New Life Matching Puzzle

Easter comes during the season of spring. In spring we see many things that remind us of new life. Match the before picture, on the left, with the picture on the right of what each of God's creations becomes.

Art: Dave Schimmell

Color the Picture

Art: Charles Jakubowski

New Life Code

Decode the message below to discover exciting news that we are to share with others.

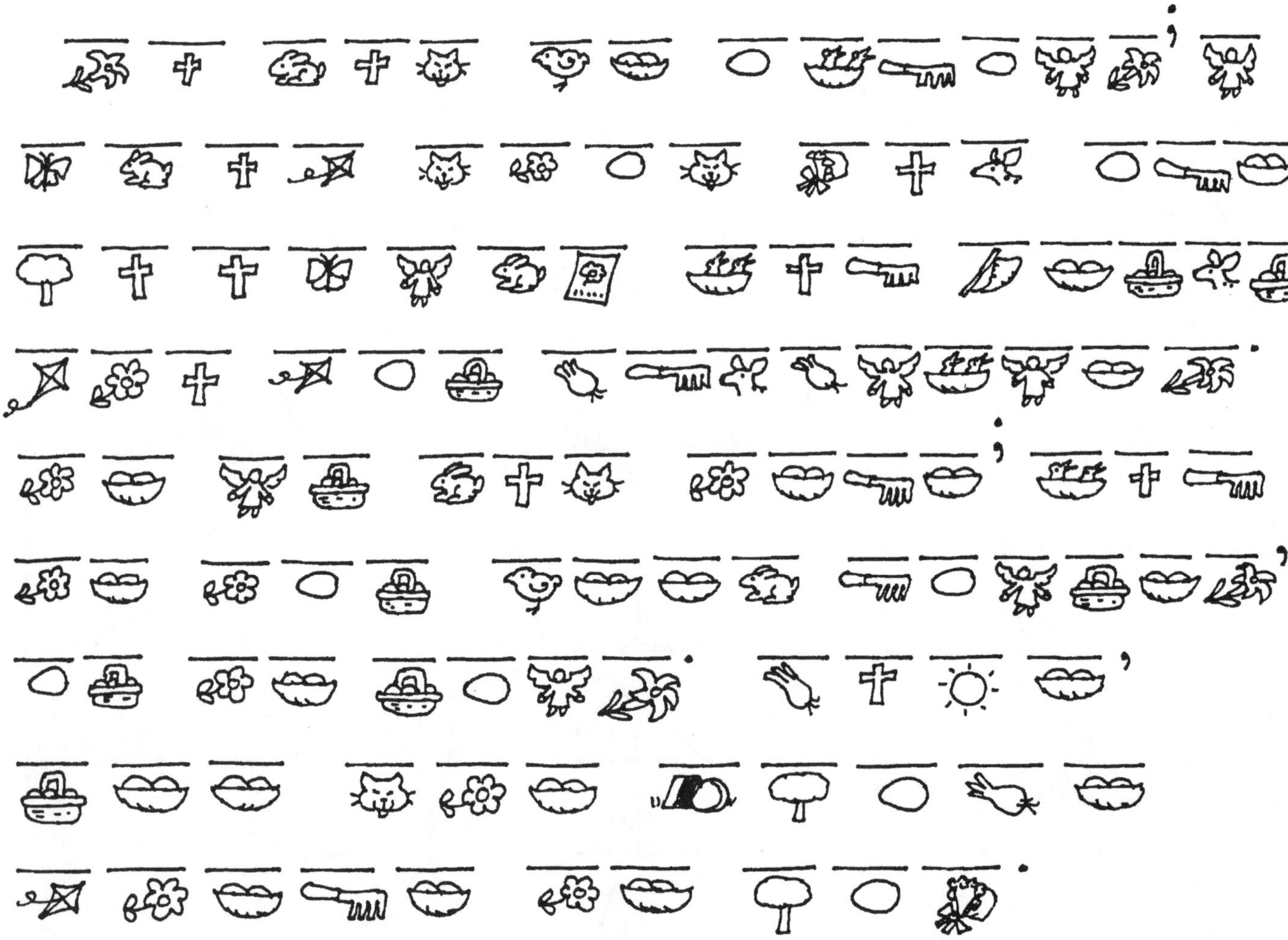

Matthew 28:5b-7

Art: Jim Padgett

Folding a Butterfly

A butterfly is a symbol of new life. A caterpillar enters a tomb (cocoon) and emerges as a butterfly. It is completely transformed to a new life.

Begin with a 6-inch square of thin paper. Wrapping paper or precut origami paper works best. Follow the instructions to fold your paper and bring a butterfly to life.

The heavier -- -- -- -- dotted line shows the fold you will be doing. The lighter - - - - - dotted line shows a fold or crease you have already done.

1. Crease paper then fold in half
2. Fold in quarter
3. Open the top flap to left
4. Turn over
5. Open the top flap to the right.
6. Fold the bottom edges up as shown so they align with lighter fold line. Leave in place (do not unfold)
7. Fold in and out to crease
8. A B Fold down and up to crease
9. Pinch A and B and fold in
10. Turn over

1

2

3

4

5

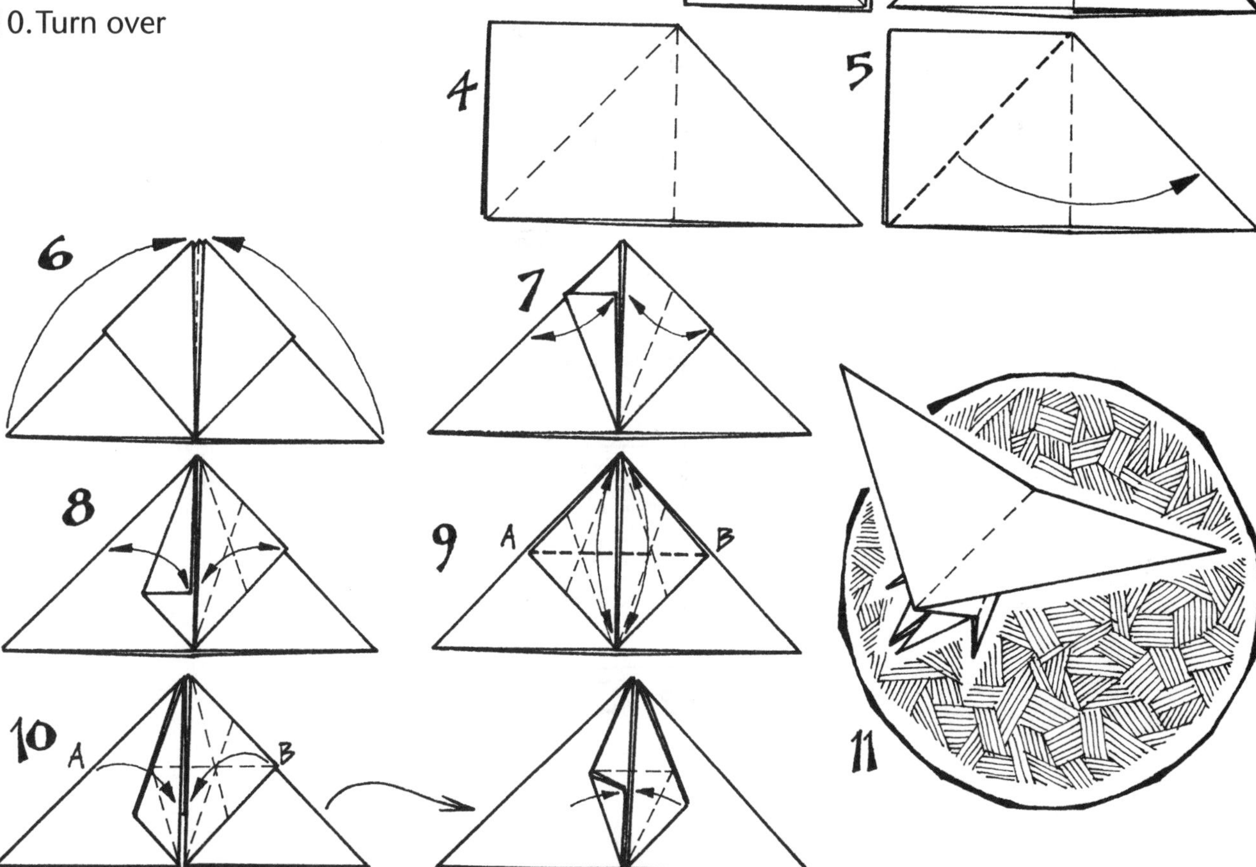

Art: Brenda Gilliam

27

Resurrection Review

If you need help, look in Mark 11:1-10; Luke 22:7-23, 39-46 (and Mark 14:32); and Matthew 28:1-10.

ACROSS

2. At Easter we celebrate Jesus' _______.
6. "Father, if you are willing, remove this ____ from me."
7. The garden where Jesus prayed.
8. Jesus is ______!
10. Jesus said he would meet his disciples here after the resurrection.
11. Jesus prayed on the Mount of ______.
12. Peter and John followed a man carrying a ________________.
13. The disciples went to _____ while Jesus prayed.
15. Jesus rode this into Jerusalem.
16. The city where Jesus was crucified and rose again.
17. "This cup is the new ________ in my blood."

DOWN

1. An _____ met the women at the tomb.
2. "This do in __________ of me."
3. The women were looking for Jesus who was _________.
4. This means "Save us!" The crowd shouted it to Jesus.
5. Mary ______ and the other Mary went to the tomb.
9. Jesus was ________ by a close friend.
10. These were posted outside Jesus' tomb.
14. Jesus shared the _________ meal with his disciples.

Spring 2005, Lesson 4

SR

Art: Jim Padgett

Leftover Easter Eggs

You will need:

eggshell pieces in a variety of colors
posterboard, white glue, pencil, scissors

Once you have found all those Easter eggs, what do you do with them? Eat them of course! Then save the shells to make a mosaic picture.

1. Cut the posterboard into a piece the size of a standard sheet of paper.

2. Choose a design that is related to Easter—butterfly, flower, cross. Lightly sketch the design onto the posterboard, providing large blocks of space for the eggshells.

3. Paint in one of the spaces with white glue.

4. Press the pieces of eggshell onto the glue. Keep the colors separate or mix them together. Do one area at a time so that the glue will not dry before the shells are placed on it.

5. Let the design dry and display your creation.

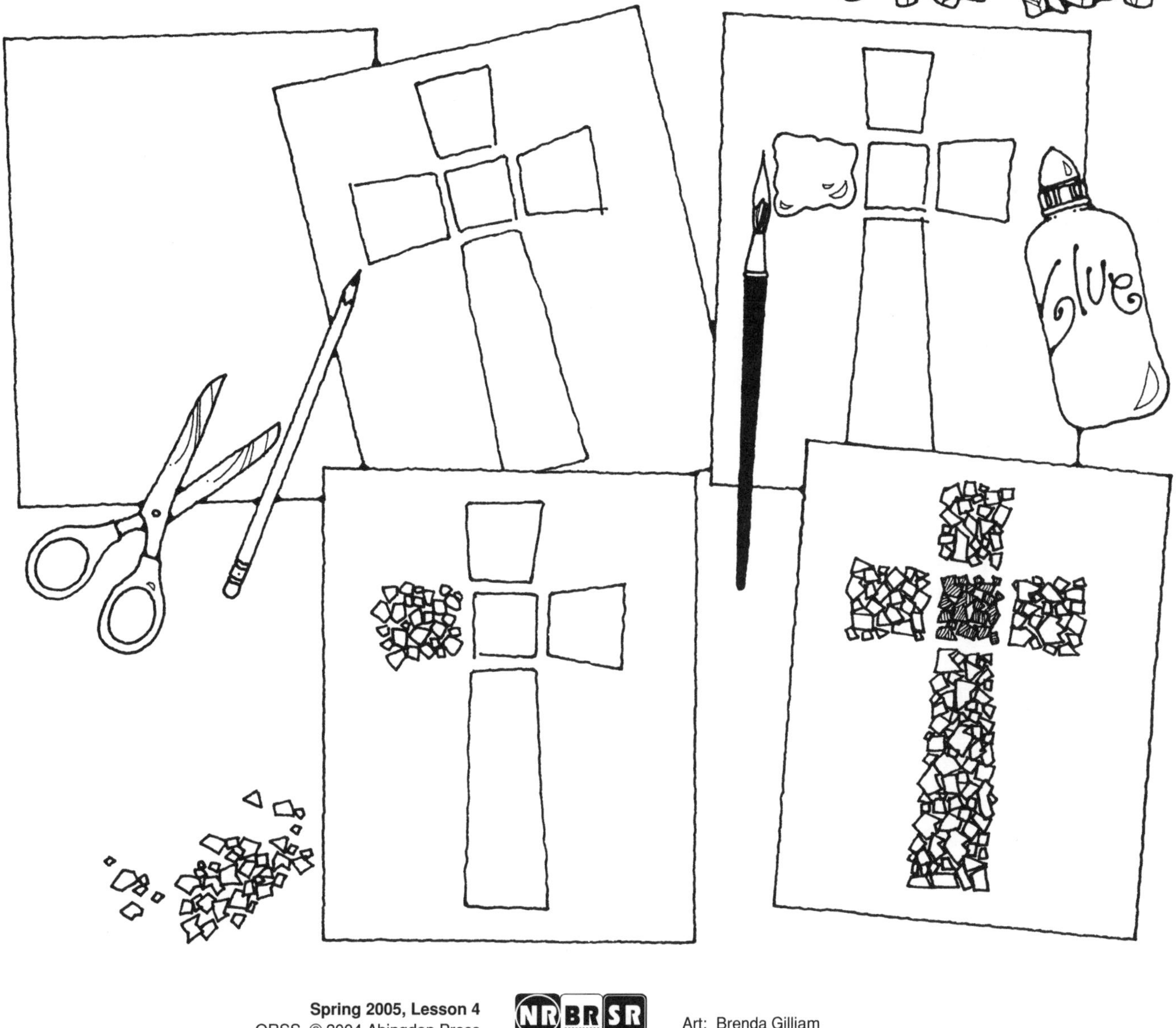

Art: Brenda Gilliam

WITNESS ON THE ROAD

Now, on that Sunday two followers of Jesus were walking on the road to Emmaus. They were talking together about all the things that had happened that week. As they talked, Jesus came and joined them, but they did not know him.

Who is that man? *(Turn to person on right)*

Who is that man? *(Turn to person on left)*

The man asked them what they were talking about. Cleopas said, "Are you only a visitor to Jerusalem? Do you not know what has happened these past few days?" The man asked, "What things?"

Who is that man? *(Turn to person on right)*

Who is that man? *(Turn to person on left)*

The two were surprised that the man did not seem to know what had happened. "About Jesus of Nazareth. He was a prophet, powerful in word and action before God and before the people. Our leaders gave him over to be crucified. Did you not hear?"

The men continued telling this stranger of all the events that had happened. "Some of the women went to the tomb this morning and could not find his body. They came and told us about seeing angels, who said Jesus was alive. And you have heard none of this?"

Who is that man? *(Turn to person on right)*

Who is that man? *(Turn to person on left)*

The men were amazed that this stranger seemed to know nothing of these events. "Some of our friends went to the tomb. They found it empty, just as the women said. But, they didn't see Jesus or angels."

Who is that man? *(Turn to person on right)*

Who is that man? *(Turn to person on left)*

Then the stranger said to them, "You are foolish and slow not to believe all the prophets spoke of. Did they not say that Christ would suffer these things and then go to be with God in glory?" Then to their amazement, this man began to tell them all the Scriptures that told about Jesus, beginning with Moses and through all the prophets.

Who is that man? *(Turn to person on right)*

Who is that man? *(Turn to person on left)*

As they approached Emmaus, the men invited the stranger to stay with them, since it was getting close to dark. So he went in with them and sat down at their table. When he was seated at the table with them, he took bread, gave thanks, broke it, and began to give it to them. It was then that the men knew who the man was!

Who is this man? *(Turn to person on right)*

THIS MAN IS JESUS!

(Turn to person on left)

Color the Picture

Art: Cary Pillo

Art: Bob Jones

Travel the Emmaus Road

Read each of the Scripture references as you move along the road. When you reach the end, hold up the sheet to a mirror and read the message.

SR
Art: Yoshi Miyake

The Cobbler

Based on a story by Leo Tolstoy, 1828-1910

There was once a cobbler named Martin. Martin was very old. His children were grown and his wife was in heaven with the Lord she loved. Martin was lonely, but he kept busy repairing shoes in his basement cobbler shop.

One night as he slept, Martin dreamed that Christ was standing before him. In his dream, Jesus said, "Tomorrow, I will visit you."

When Martin awoke the next morning the dream was still so real that he was convinced it was a message from the Lord. He was sure that on this very day, Christ would appear before him. Martin wanted everything at its best for such a special visitor. He spread evergreen boughs around the room, swept the floor, and washed down the walls. Even as he worked, he kept glancing out his window at the feet passing by on the street above. There were tired feet and young, running feet, but no holy sandals of the Christ.

"When Jesus arrives, I must have something to serve him," thought the cobbler. So he baked bread and simmered apple cider on the stove. Soon the room smelled heavenly with the aroma of freshly baked bread and apples and cinnamon. But to Martin's disappointment there was no heavenly appearance.

As the bread was baking, Martin glanced repeatedly out the window. He saw the worn boots of an old man. They were patched and scuffed. The man shuffled unsteadily as he walked. Martin opened his door and saw that the boots were worn by an old soldier. Martin called after him, "Please come in. It is such a chilly day, and I would welcome your company over a cup of cider." Slowly the old man turned and climbed down the stairs to Martin's shop. Together they passed a pleasant hour in silence, each appreciating the warmth of the cider and the company.

As the man was leaving, Martin heard shouts and the scuffle of feet. A street vendor was chasing after a little boy, grabbing him by his ragged shirt, "You thief, you dirty little thief," yelled the shopkeeper. Martin hurried up his stairs. "Whatever the trouble is here, I am sure it can soon be made right," he said.

"This boy stole three apples!" exclaimed the vendor. Martin reached in his pocket and pulled out some coins. "Here, now you have your money for the apples."

Turning to the boy, Martin said, "Come, apples always taste better with freshly baked bread."

So Martin and the boy returned to the warmth of the shop. When the boy had eaten his fill, Martin sent him on his way with a bundle of apples and nuts and bread.

By now, daylight was fading. Martin stared out the window. He had been so sure that his dream was real. Where was Christ? Oh, how he longed to welcome his Lord. Of course, it wouldn't be quite the welcome he'd planned. The bread was half gone, the warm cider too. The floor was no longer spotless. There were scuffs on the floor from the little boy and bits of mud from the old soldier's boots.

Outside his window few feet passed. Then he saw the bent shadow of a young woman clutching a child. The woman's feet moved slowly, as if she barely had the strength to carry on. Martin looked at the remaining bread and cider. He opened his door and called up to the woman. Soon she was huddled by his fire, eating the last of the food he had prepared for this Special Guest.

Before letting the woman head off into the night, Martin went to a trunk in the corner and pulled out a shawl worn by his late wife and a blanket that once wrapped his own child. Putting the shawl over the woman's shoulders and handing her the blanket, he saw the pair on their way.

Sadly, Martin stood at his window as night fell. The day was gone and Christ had not appeared. Kneeling in prayer, Martin cried, "Lord, I so wanted to meet you today. I wanted to serve you, to fill your cup, to break bread with you, to offer you shelter. Why didn't you come? Was it all just a dream?"

Then, to Martin's surprise, a voice answered, "I visited you three times today and all three times you took care of my needs. I was the old soldier, the hungry boy, and the young mother."

"Remember my words and know that whatever you do to the least of these, you have done to me."

35 COLOR BY SYMBOL

Color each shape according to the symbol in that shape. (Any color will do as long as all of the symbols are the same color.) *See what is revealed when you are finished!*

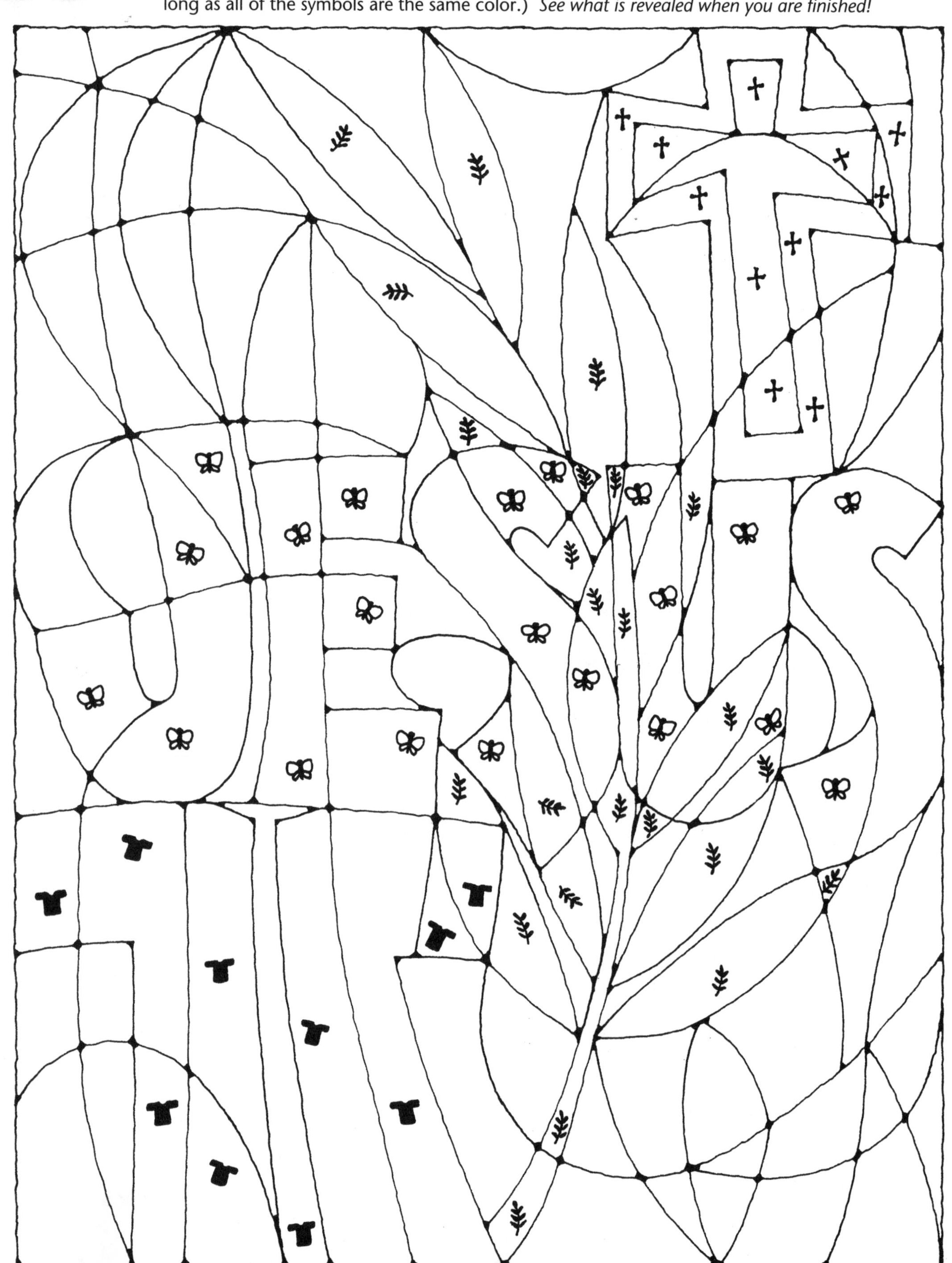

SR

Art: Brenda Gilliam

I Have Seen Jesus!

MARY MAGDALENE: I had told the twelve all that happened at the tomb, that I saw Jesus.

JAMES: But of course, we really didn't believe her. We were afraid of our Jewish leaders. Judas had plotted with them to turn Jesus over to them.

ANDREW: It was the day after the sabbath. We had gathered together.

PHILIP: And locked the door for safety!

JAMES: Yes, we were afraid of what might happen to us now that Jesus had been crucified.

PHILIP: When suddenly, Jesus was there with us.

ANDREW: He held out his hands to show the nail marks in his hands. We saw the spear wound in his side.

PHILIP: We were amazed!

ANDREW: We were all so happy. We were no longer afraid!

JAMES: Jesus spoke to us, "I'm sending you like God sent me. Receive the Holy Spirit."

PHILIP: He breathed on us—like God breathed on the dust and gave Adam life. It was totally amazing!

JAMES: Thomas wasn't with us that night, although he was one of the twelve.

ANDREW: *(sadly)* Eleven by then.

PHILIP: So, later we said to him, "We've seen the Lord!"

ANDREW: Thomas was still afraid; he didn't believe us.

THOMAS: I told them, "First, I must see his hands and his side. I must see the place where the spear cut his side. Then I'll believe you saw Jesus here in this room!"

ANDREW: The next week we again gathered together.

THOMAS: This time I was there.

PHILIP: Again the doors were locked. But again, Jesus was just there. He was just standing there.

THOMAS: Jesus greeted me with my own challenge, "Put your finger here in the mark of the nail, your hand here in my side."

JAMES: "Stop doubting; have faith," Jesus said.

THOMAS: I fell to my knees. I believed. Jesus is my Lord and my God!

MARY MAGDALENE: Jesus worked many signs to show that he was the Son of God. Some are written down so that you will put your faith in Jesus as the chosen one of God. If you put your faith in him, you will have true life!

Based on John 20:19-31
Written by Nancy Hollobaugh Gain

Color the Picture

NR

Art: Jim Padgett

Believe It!

Read each of the headlines below. Five are true. Three are not.
Glue an "I Believe" circle beside the ones you believe to be true.

1. Martians Land in New York City!
2. Bosco, a Black Labrador Retriever, Is Elected Mayor of Sunol, CA.
3. Elephant Clocked Tiptoeing Down the Road at 25 Miles Per Hour.
4. Spider Gets Stuck in Its Own Web.
5. Hamster Found After Two Years, Living in Family Sofa.
6. Romanian Man Strikes Oil as He Digs Hole to Plant Tree.
7. Man in Crane Costume Leads Lost Sand Hill Cranes to Wildlife Preserve.
8. Chicken Lays Egg the Shape of Italy.

Some things are easy to believe. Some things are hard to believe.
As Christians we believe that **Jesus is God's Son.**

Art: Dennis Jones

A Message of Faith

YOU WILL NEED:

a white candle ***(birthday candles work well)***
or a white crayon
white construction paper
watercolor paints, water, and a brush

Using the crayon or candle as a pen, decorate a 1-inch border around the outside edge of your paper with symbols of faith.

On the center of the paper, write "**BELIEVE**" in bold letters. Press firmly with the wax candle to leave wax on the paper.

Use watercolor paints to cover all the paper. Use as many colors as you like. The pictures and symbols drawn in the wax or crayon will remain white and reveal your message of faith.

Art: Brenda Gilliam

The disciples were frightened after Jesus' crucifixion. They were afraid the Jewish leaders might come after them next. So they went into hiding. But someone found them. Read John 20:19.

Who found them?

What did he say to them?

Mark out all the Xs, Zs, Qs, Vs, and Ks.

Art: Yoshi Miyake

41

MATCH BIBLE VERSES

Some verses hold more than one sentence or idea. When we look for a thought that sums up an idea, we often look at part of a verse. Using part of a verse helps focus our attention to the one idea we're thinking about.

When you are looking at one of the ideas in a verse, it may be marked with a lower case *a* or *b* to show where in the verse the words are found.

Match the beginnings of the following verses with their ending and draw a line to the correct scripture reference.

So the other disciples told him, "We have seen the Lord."	Jesus came and stood among them and said, "Peace be with you."	**John 20:19**
When it was evening on that day, the first day of the week, and the doors of the house where the disciples had met were locked for fear of the Jews	"if you retain the sins of any, they are retained."	**John 20:23**
A week later his disciples were again in the house, and Thomas was with them. Although the doors were shut,	But he said to them, "Unless I see the mark of the nails in his hands, and put my finger in the mark of the nails and my hand in his side, I will not believe."	**John 20:25**
		John 20:26
Jesus said to him, "Have you believed because you have seen me?"	Jesus came and stood among them and said, "Peace be with you."	**John 20:29**
"If you forgive the sins of any they are forgiven them"	"Blessed are those who have not seen and yet have come to believe."	

When do you doubt?

Jesus said, **"Do not doubt but believe."**

Thomas wanted to be sure the good news the other disciples shared with him was true. Jesus had been put to death. Thomas was frightened; he had doubts.

Think of times when you need to remember,
"Do not doubt but believe."

Write them in the space below. Then bring your page to the closing worship to share with your friends.

SR

Art: Jim Padgett

43 A Good Night for Fishing

Peter and his friends had had a very unusual few days. First their friend and teacher had been put to death on a cross. They were frightened and sad. Then they heard the best news of all, Jesus was alive once more. Jesus even went to see them and one of them, Thomas, had touched Jesus on the places where he had been wounded. But now they didn't really know what to do. Should they go on teaching others about Jesus and about God's love, or should they wait for awhile?

Finally, Peter said, "I'm going fishing."

"We will go too," the others replied.

Jesus' first disciples, Peter, Andrew, James, and John, made their living as fishermen. Others had grown up on the shore of Lake Galilee and understood about boats and fishing. They thought this would be a good way to spend some time as they thought about what they would do with their lives now.

In Bible times fishing was done mainly in the evening or early morning when the fish tended to be nearer the surface. So on this night the men went out in a boat, dropping heavy nets over the sides and pulling them back in. But as dawn approached they had caught no fish.

As the sun rose, they looked toward the shore and saw a man standing on the beach.

The man was Jesus, but the fishermen did not recognize him. He called to them, "Friends, have you caught any fish?"

"No!" they replied.

Then Jesus said a strange thing. He told them to throw out their nets on the right hand side of the boat. "You will catch plenty of fish if you do," he said.

The disciples did as Jesus had told them, and their net was filled with fish! In fact the net was so full they couldn't drag it back into the boat.

That was when one of the disciples realized who the man on the shore was. "It's Jesus!" he exclaimed. Peter grabbed his tunic and jumped into the water. The others brought the boat in with the full nets dragging behind it. When they all got to the shore, they saw that Jesus had lit a fire and was frying fish. There was good fresh bread to eat with the fish.

Jesus told them to bring some more of the fish they had caught so there would be plenty for all. They counted 153 large fish.

Then Jesus himself served them a breakfast of bread and fish.

1. Color the fish and cut it out.
2. Divide the fish into three parts by cutting along the dotted lines.
3. Punch out the nine black dots.
4. Thread yarn through the holes to put the fish loosely back together as shown. Tape the loose ends of the yarn on the back of the fish.
5. Tie a long piece of yarn through the hole near the fish's mouth. Tie the other end of the yarn to a dowel.

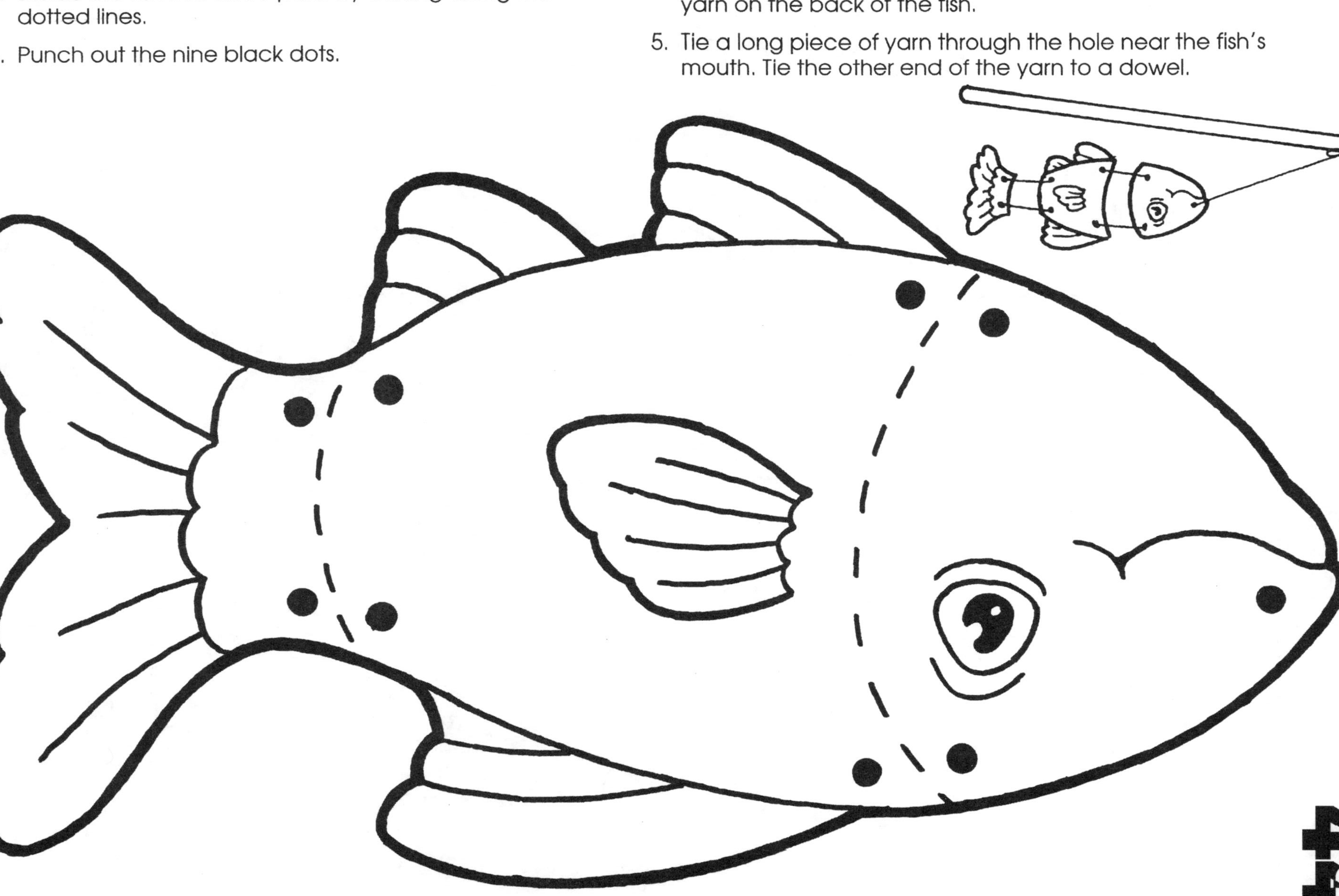

Art: Sherry Neidigh

Color the Picture

NR
Art: Jim Padgett

1. Choose one fish.
2. Find a second fish exactly like the one fish you have chosen.
3. Color the two fish the same color.
4. Choose a third fish. Then find a matching fish. Color these two fish a second color.
5. Continue until all the matching pairs of fish are a different color.

How many pairs of matching fish can you find?

Art: Ron LeHew

47 Scrimshaw Jewelry

Many years ago people made jewelry by carving pictures into ivory and bones from large mammals such as whales. The jewelry was called scrimshaw. Make a scrimshaw fish to remind you that God helped Jonah and that God is willing to help us when we have to make hard choices and do hard tasks. We do not use ivory or animal bones today, but you can use clay dough.

Make the Clay Dough

1 cup cold water
1 cup salt
2 teaspoons oil
3 cups flour
2 tablespoons cornstarch
food coloring in several colors

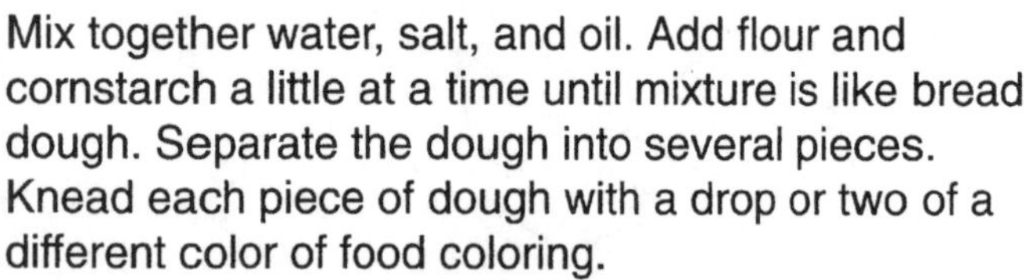

Mix together water, salt, and oil. Add flour and cornstarch a little at a time until mixture is like bread dough. Separate the dough into several pieces. Knead each piece of dough with a drop or two of a different color of food coloring.

Make the Scrimshaw Fish

1. Shape a fish from the clay dough. Use several colors to make your fish interesting.
2. Use a pencil to make a hole where the fish's eye would be.
3. Make designs on the fish with the point of the pencil.
4. Let your fish design dry. (You may have to wait a few days for your fish to dry.)
5. Thread yarn through the fish's eye to make a necklace, bracelet, or key chain.

Spring 2005, Lesson 7
ORSS, © 2004 Abingdon Press

Art: Megan Jeffery

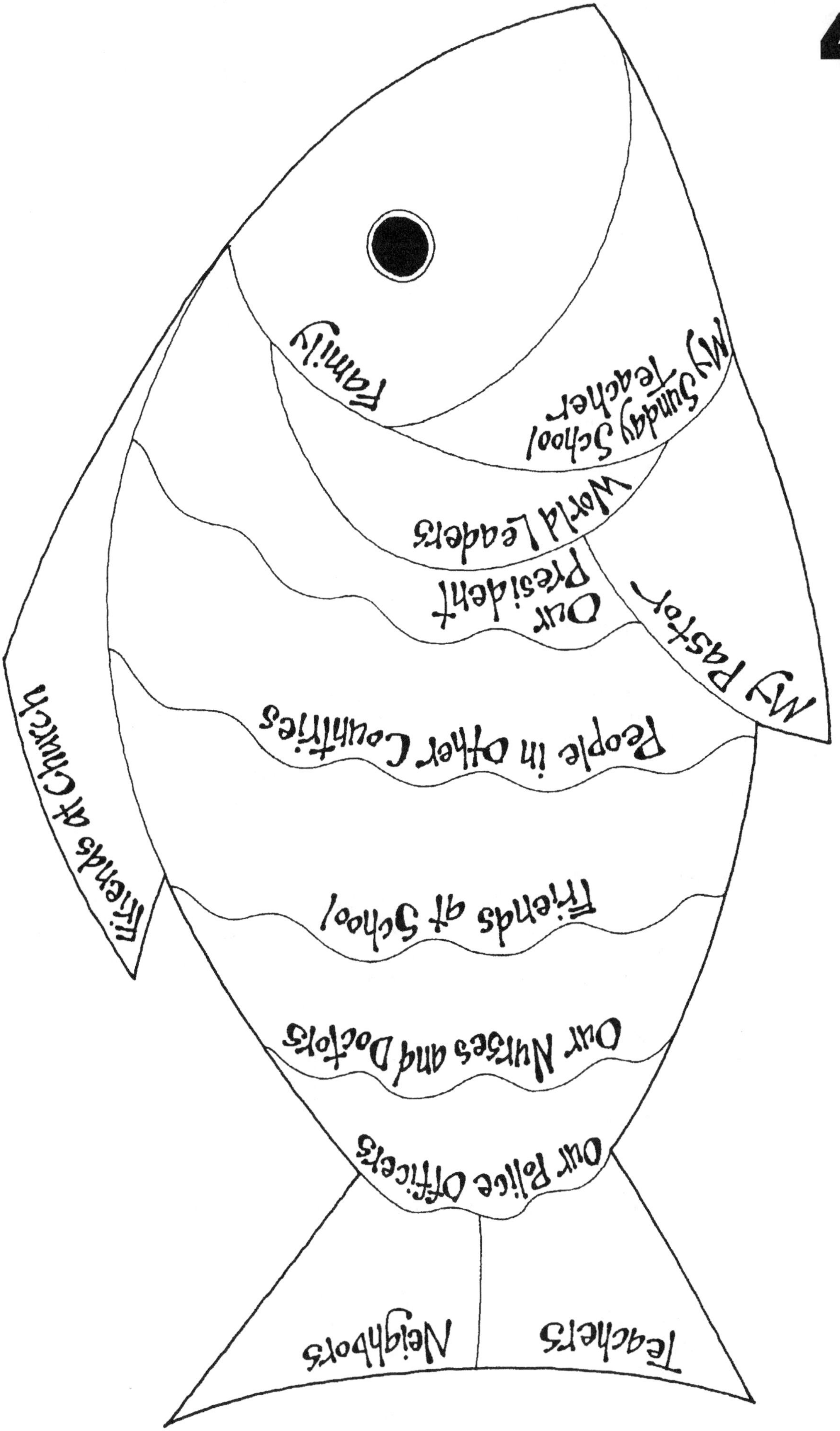

Family

My Sunday School Teacher

World Leaders

Our President

My Pastor

Friends at Church

People in Other Countries

Friends at School

Our Nurses and Doctors

Our Police Officers

Neighbors

Teachers

Art: Brenda Gilliam

Practicing Faithfulness

Spiritual disciplines are not punishment. Instead, spiritual disciplines are a way to practice the habits that can help us grow in our relationship with God or become more like Jesus.

Four of the many spiritual disciplines are listed here. Read the descriptions. Then choose one of the spiritual discipline activities that you will practice this week.

Service

A servant looks for opportunities to help others. Jesus gave us an example of servanthood when he washed the disciples' feet (John 13:1-17). A servant thinks of others rather than thinking only of self.

Activity for the Week: Choose a place in your community where you can be of service to others. Or do a chore for someone in your family without being asked.

Prayer

Prayer is a special way to communicate with God. Prayer involves both listening to God and talking to God. We pray for others, or we pray for ourselves. When we pray, we praise God, we give thanks, we confess our sins, and we ask for forgiveness and help.

Activity for the Week: Set aside a special time to pray every day. Pray for your family and for your friends. Close with the Lord's Prayer each day.

Study

Study includes reading the Bible and other books that help us understand God's Word. The discipline of study helps us understand more about God and ourselves.

Activity for the Week: Read something from the Bible each day. Think about what the verses you read teach you about living as a faithful Christian.

Worship

Worship is a time to praise God. Worship is a time to recognize that God is with us and to sense God's presence. We can worship by singing, praying, or giving thanks. We can worship alone, or we can worship with others.

Activity for the Week: Choose a special place to worship God in private. Sing or pray your own songs and prayers. Then worship God with others by being in church on Sunday morning.

Art: Sherry Neidigh

Jesus had been raised from the dead and appeared to his disciples twice. Now for a third time, Jesus appeared to Peter and some of the other disciples while they were fishing. He cooked breakfast for them on the beach and served it to them. Afterwards, while they were sitting quietly on the shore, Jesus spoke to Peter.

"Peter," Jesus said, "do you love me?"

Peter was astonished. Surely Jesus knew how much he loved him! "Yes, Lord," he answered quickly. "You know I love you."

"Then feed my lambs," Jesus said. And then Jesus repeated the question. "Simon Peter, son of John, do you love me?"

"Yes, Lord," Peter answered. "You know I love you."

"Then take care of my sheep," Jesus said. And once again he repeated the question, "Peter, do you love me?"

Peter was near tears. He cried out, "Lord, you know everything, so you must know that I love you."

And one more time Jesus answered, "Feed my sheep."

Perhaps Peter thought back to the times that Jesus had referred to himself as the good shepherd. He knew that Jesus loved all the people who gathered around to hear him teach and who followed him around the countryside. He cared for them when they were hurt or ill. He arranged food for them when they were hungry. And he told them that they must do the same for others. And more—they must visit those who were sick or in prison, they must give clothes to those who needed clothes. And Peter realized that Jesus was telling him that he would have to care for others the way Jesus had cared for them—as carefully as a shepherd cared for lambs and sheep.

Maybe Peter remembered that three times he had denied he knew Jesus. Now Jesus had questioned him three times about love. Peter had answered three times that he loved Jesus and three times Jesus had reminded him to show that love to others.

Later someone wrote this story down to remind Jesus' followers in the early church to care for others. Today as we read it, it reminds us that we too must be shepherds to those who need us.

Art: Jim Padgett

Hi! my name is David Etienne.

I live in Port-au-Prince, Haiti. I am 7 years old. I live with my mother, father, six brothers, and one sister. My mother stays home to care for us. My father goes to work at a factory.

Last year I became very ill. My mother took me to Grace Children's Hospital where a doctor did many tests. He told my mother that I had tuberculosis and severe malnutrition. That meant that I had not been getting enough good food to eat and that I had become weak. Once I was weak, it was hard for my system to fight off the tuberculosis.

I had to stay at Grace Children's Hospital for several months. Now I look and feel much better. When anyone asks about my illness, I tell them, "I was very swollen and sick when I came here. But look at me now. I am very different! I love to have fun and make the other children laugh."

Grace Children's Hospital, in Port-au-Prince, Haiti, was started in 1967 to take care of children who have tuberculosis. Children stay in one of the hospital's 72 beds for about three months to get better from the disease. When they are well enough they can go home, but they still must go back to the hospital clinic for more medicine. The extra visits help the hospital workers make sure the disease stays out of the children's bodies. About 4000 people visit the clinic each month.

Tuberculosis is very contagious. It is a disease that attacks the lungs and makes it difficult to breathe. Some people die from the disease. Many people in Haiti, including children, suffer from malnutrition.

The hospital is supported by many churches. What does your church do to help children like David?

Start in the center. Follow the three paths to find ways you can share.

What Can I Share?

BR

Art: Nell Fisher

Color the Picture

Art: Jim Padgett

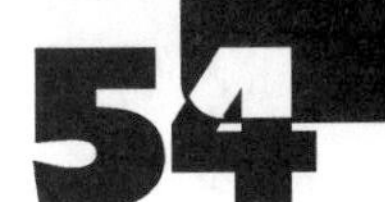

Put a check mark (✔) beside each thing you actually have.
Underline each thing you really need;
it would be hard to live without it.
Circle each thing people in a poor country really need;
they could not live without it.

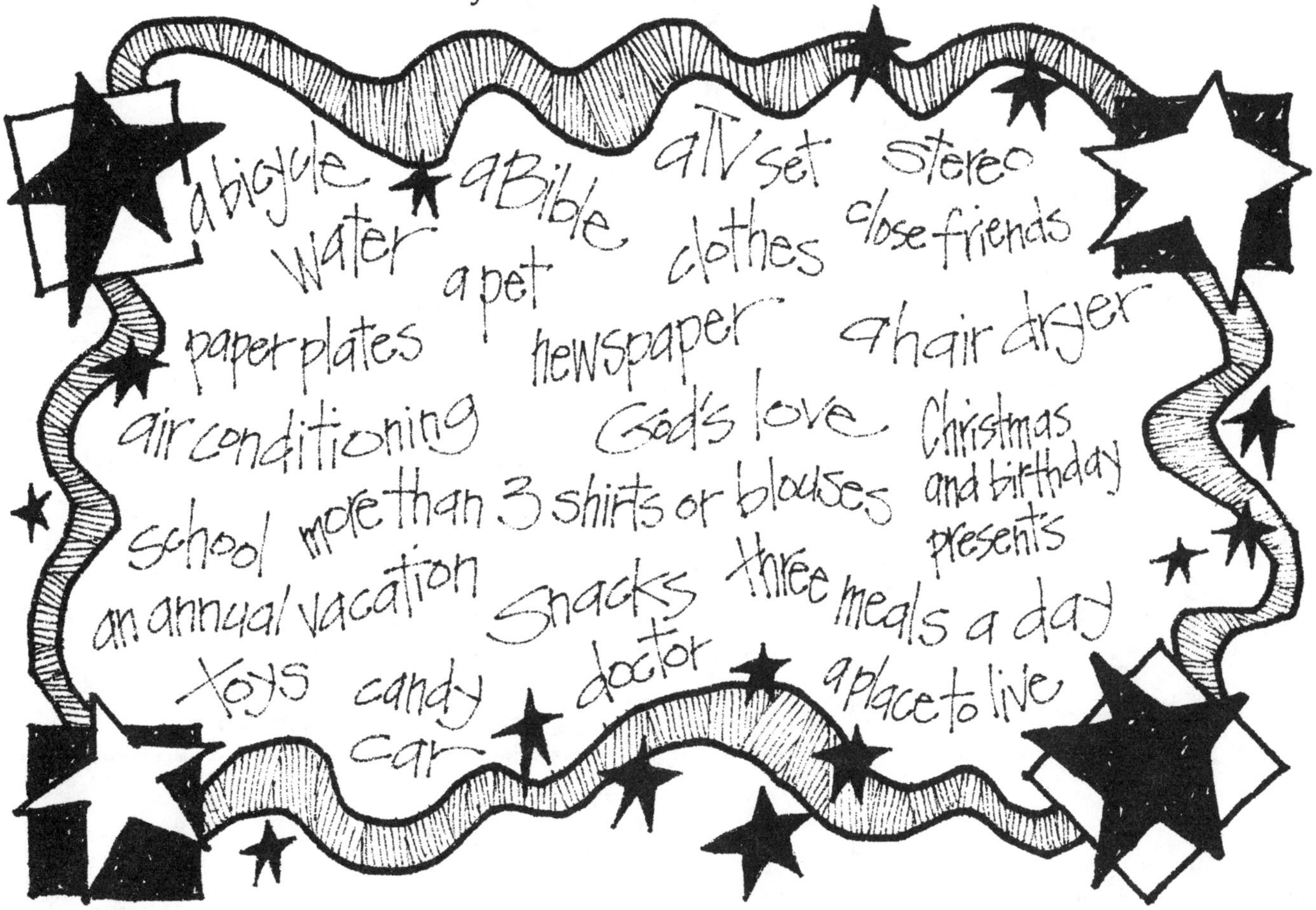

a bicycle
a Bible
a TV set
stereo
water
clothes
close friends
a pet
paper plates
newspaper
a hair dryer
air conditioning
God's love
Christmas and birthday presents
school
more than 3 shirts or blouses
an annual vacation
snacks
three meals a day
toys
candy
doctor
a place to live
car

List 1
List the things you underlined but do not have circled.

___

___

___

List 2
List the things you have checked but do not have underlined or circled.

___

___

___

Which three things from List 2 would be hardest for you to give up?

1. ___
2. ___
3. ___

Which three things from List 2 would be easiest for you to give up?

1. ___
2. ___
3. ___

Art: Brenda Gilliam

Reasons for Sharing

BR SR
Art: Bob Jones

Gifts for Sharing

Art: Bob Jones

This is what Jesus might have said if he had remained on earth to see and talk to us today. He tells us about the time he spent with his disciples in Galilee after he rose from the dead. Jesus had some very important things to tell them.

My disciples, who were my followers and dear friends, were very happy to see me again. They met me in Galilee, as I told Mary and Mary Magdalene. Some of the disciples doubted at first that I was really with them. After all, they knew I had been crucified and killed and my body put in a tomb. However, we had a wonderful time together in worship and thankfulness that I had defeated death in rising from the dead. At this meeting, I had some very important words of encouragement for my friends. I told them, "All power in heaven and on earth has been given to me. Go to all peoples everywhere and make them my disciples. Baptize them in the name of the Father and of the Son and of the Holy Spirit. Teach these new disciples to obey all the commands I have given you. And, be sure of this, I will be with you always, even to the end of the world."

It is now up to my disciples, all who love me and follow my commandments, to go tell people everywhere about God's love and my victory over death. All people need to know that I love them and that by believing in me they can have eternal life.

Remember, I will never leave you alone. I have sent the Spirit to stay with my friends always: to teach you, encourage you, and give you peace.

Based on Matthew 28:16-20
Susan D. Finehout

Go Into All the World!

Followers of Jesus did what he told them to do. Today there are more than 1,400,000,000 people all over the world who believe that Jesus is God's Son. People who believe in Jesus want to make a difference in the world.

Archbishop Desmond Tutu fought against the unfair treatment of his people in South Africa. In 1984, he won a Nobel Peace Prize for his work in bringing about peace in South Africa.

Rigoberta Menchu, a native of Guatemala, was awarded the Nobel Peace Prize in 1992 because of her work for the rights of the native Guatemalans.

Mother Teresa of Calcutta cared for the poor and dying in India until her own death.

Five children from Tennessee began saving their money so that "Other kids can be as blessed as we have been." They presented a love offering to their church in the amount of $1,035.

What difference can you make?

Art: Terry Sirrell

59 Color this picture.

Art: Benton Mahan

As disciples of Jesus we are told to tell the good news to whom?

Follow the color guide.

1 = black 4 = any color you choose

2 = blue

3 = green

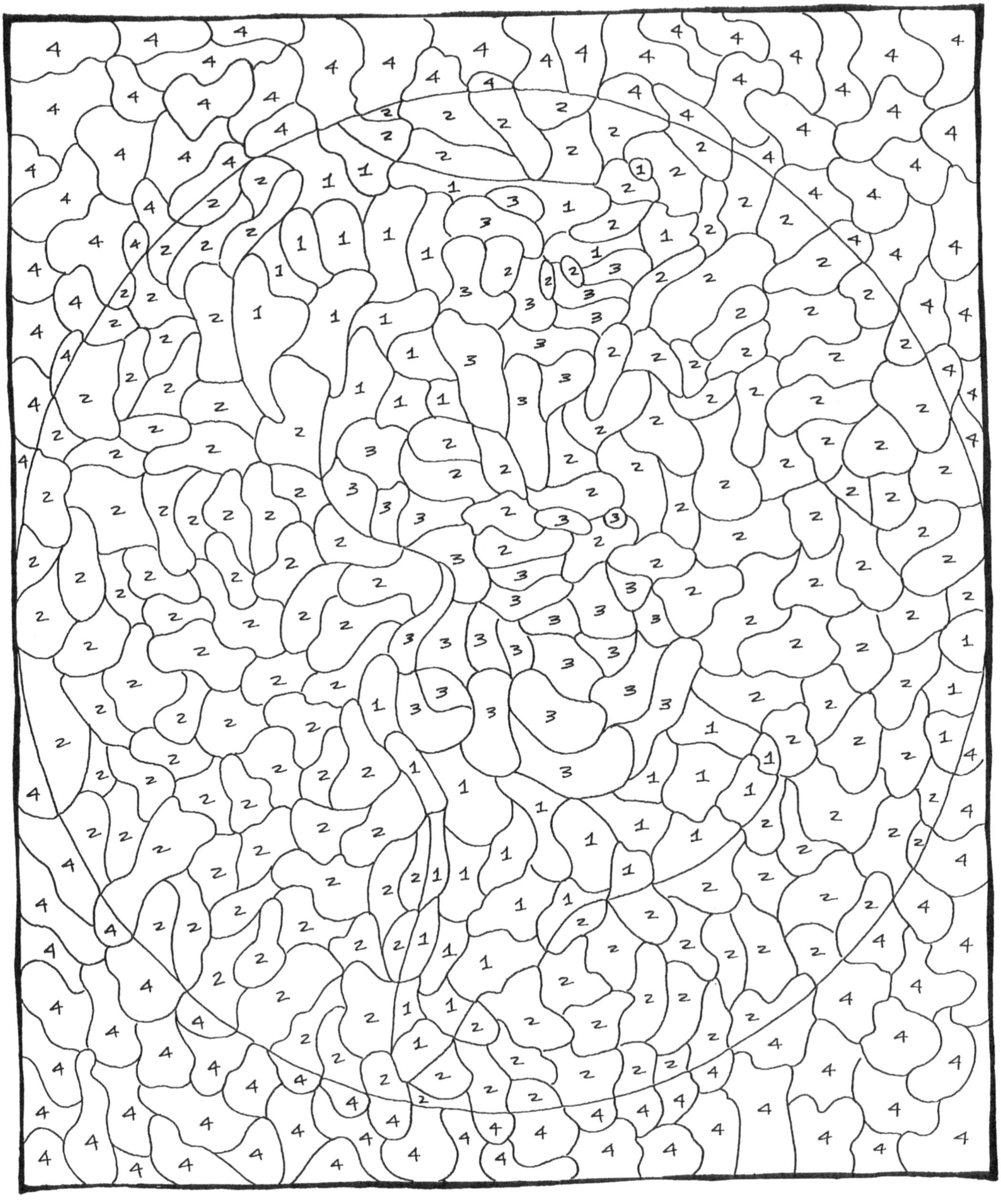

Art: Megan Jeffery

Make a Bead Cross

YOU WILL NEED:

18-inch leather shoelaces
6 pony beads per cross

1. Begin with an 18-inch leather shoelace. Thread the shoelace with one pony bead. Move the bead to the center point.

2. Thread both ends of the lace through a single bead. Push snugly against the first bead.

3. Thread the right lace through another bead, the left lace through a fourth bead, then thread the two ends through a fifth bead.

4. As you pull the lace tight, insert a sixth bead between the two side beads. Push down snugly to hold the interior bead in place.

5. Tie the ends together.

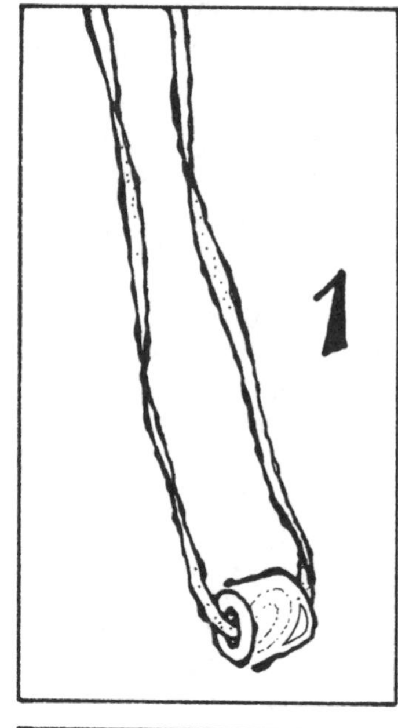

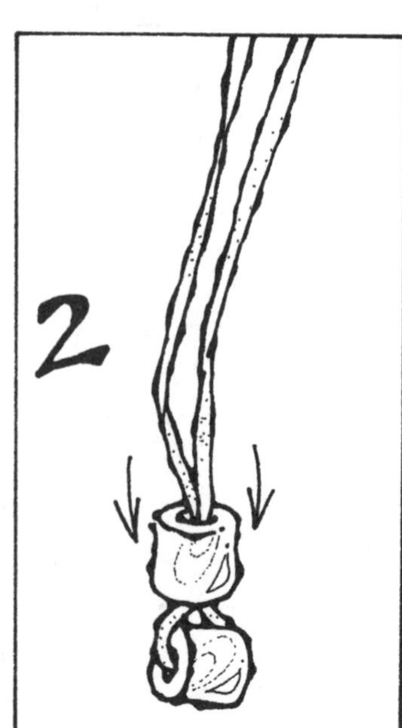

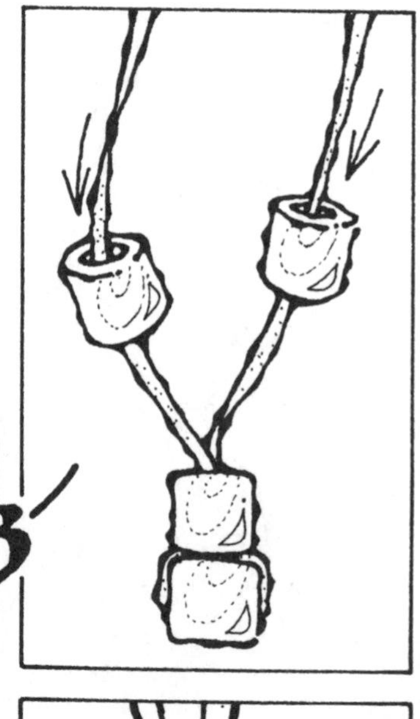

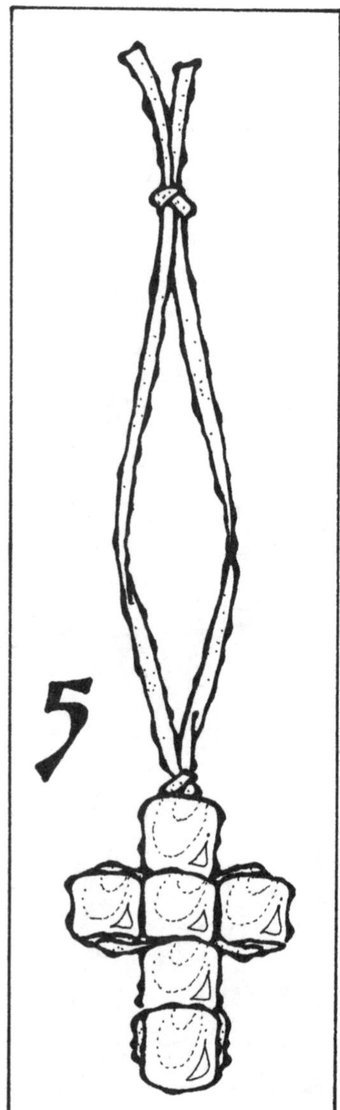

Art: Brenda Gilliam

The Great Commission Review

For help to choose the correct answers, check **Matthew 28:16-20**.

Match each empty answer box with a box on the other side of the page, so that the ends fit together like a lock and key. Choose the correct answer of the three given and write it in the empty answer box to complete the sentence.

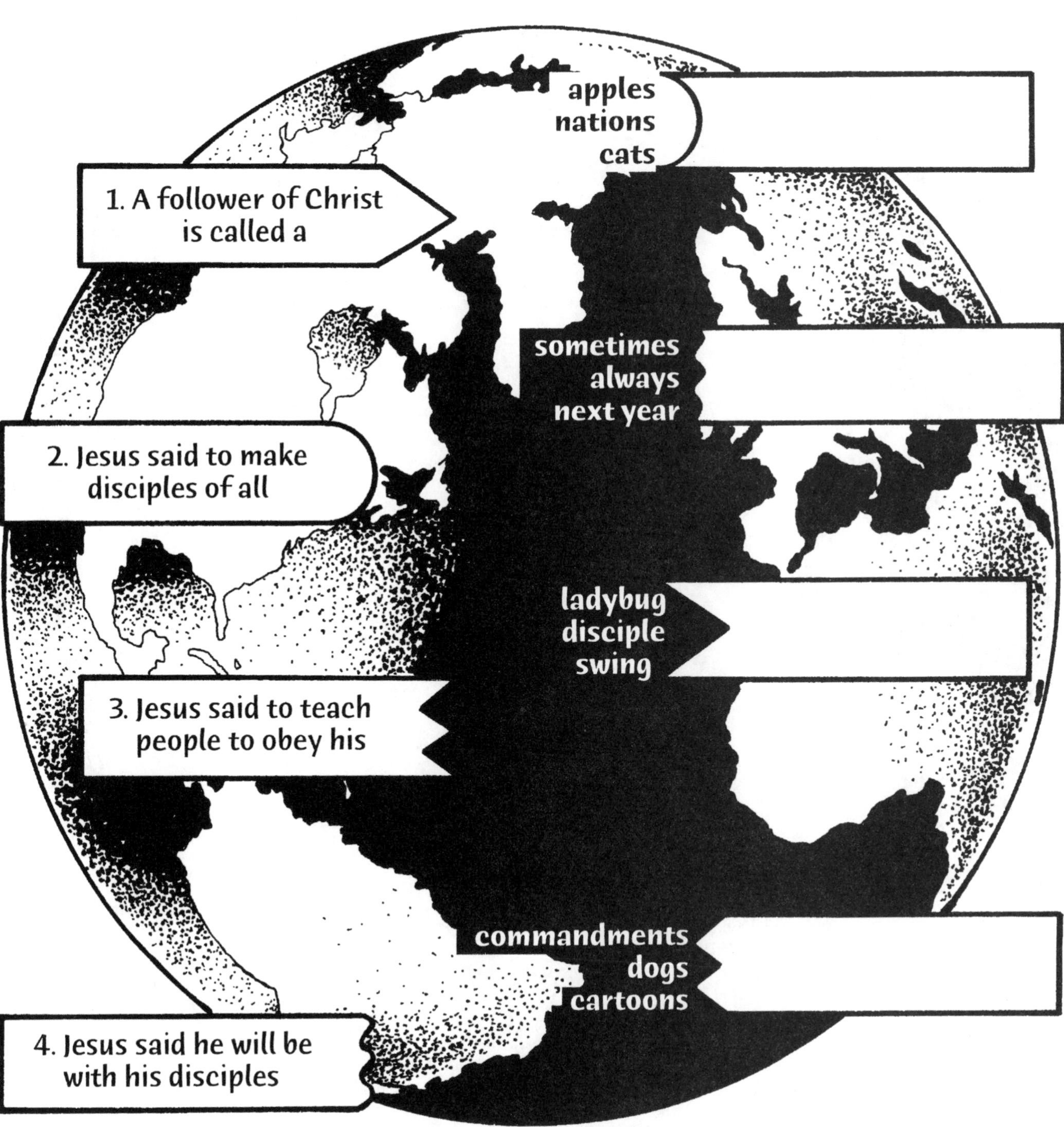

BR
Art: John Jordan

Journal Lesson 9

What does the good news mean to you?

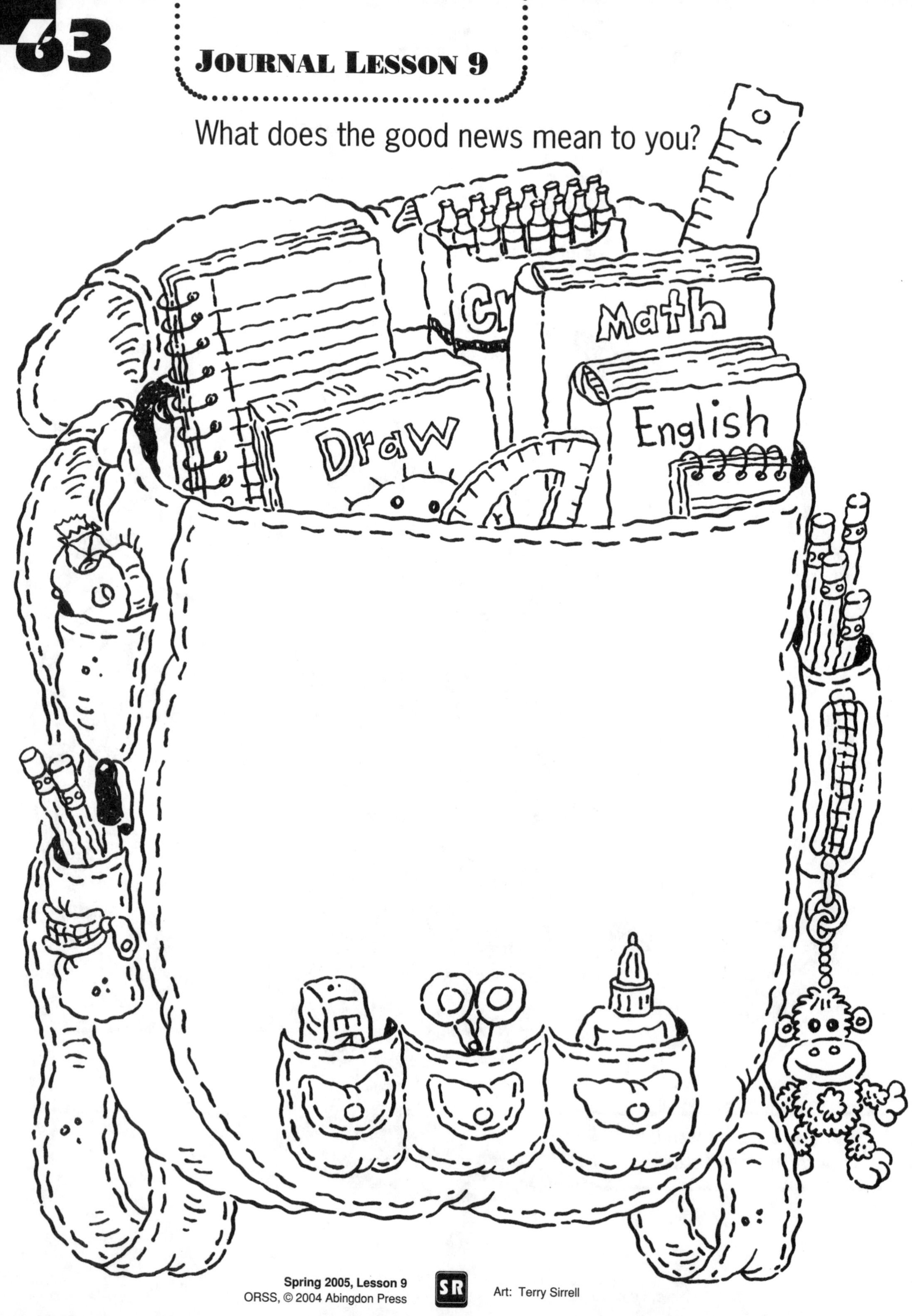

A Gift Greater Than Gold!

Today I received a special gift—a gift greater than any gold or silver. Today, after forty years, I can walk! Let me tell you the story.

Every day some friends would carry me to the Beautiful Gate. There I would sit all day. I sat because I could not stand. I sat because I could not walk. I sat because there was nothing else I could do.

I would sit at the Beautiful Gate watching the people walk past me on their way to the Temple. I would ask the people for money to buy food as they passed by, so that I could live. Since I could not walk, I could not work.

Today, about three o'clock in the afternoon as people hurried by on their way to the Temple to pray, I called out, "Alms for the poor. Help a man who cannot walk." Most people ignored me as usual and hurried on their way. But two men stopped. I held out my hand, expecting to receive the coins I was sure they would give me.

But one of the men took my hand and said, "Look at me! I don't have any silver or gold to give you. But I do have another gift. In the name of Jesus, stand up and walk."

At the moment he spoke the words, "in the name of Jesus," I felt the strength return to my legs. It began with my toes and worked its way up to my ankles, then my knees. I jumped to my feet! I began to walk! I began to jump! I began to dance! As I walked and jumped and danced, I also shouted praises to God. I was lame no longer.

I followed the two men into the Temple, walking and jumping and praising. All the people there knew me. They had seen me many times as they hurried past. But today I was walking, and they were amazed. They didn't understand how this could happen.

I was happy. But when the priests and the Sadducees heard what had happened, they were annoyed. They simply couldn't allow these two men to continue preaching and teaching in the name of Jesus Christ! So the priests sent guards to find the men and arrest them.

Then the two men were brought before the council. I wasn't at the council meeting, but I heard about what happened. The council ordered the two to stop what they were doing. But this didn't work. In fact one of the men spoke up boldly and said, "Even if it means going to prison, my friend and I cannot help but speak out about what we have seen and heard."

The council couldn't decide what to do with the two, so they let them go. And the two men continued to speak boldly about Jesus wherever they went.

(Based on Acts 3:1-21)
Linda Crooks

Color the picture

NR

Art: Megan Jeffery

I Can Help others

Draw a circle around the things you can do to help others. Can you think of other ways to help?

NR BR

Art: Yoshi Miyake

Read Acts 4:16-20

In today's Bible story the council tells Peter and John that they must stop doing something. Put a checkmark beside the pictures of those things that the council has said Peter and John must stop doing.

BR SR

Art: Terry Sirrell

The Lame Begger

Read the story in Acts 3:1-10 and 4:1-21.
Then use the information you find to finish this crossword puzzle.

ACROSS

1. The name of the gate (3:2)
4. "The stone the builders rejected has become the ________." (4:11)
6. The other disciple with John (3:1)
7. "I have no _______ or gold." (3:6)
9. The man was walking and leaping and praising ______. (3:9)

DOWN

2. The high priest at the time. (4:6)
3. The time of day (3:1)
4. Former high priest who was present (4:6)
5. Jesus' hometown (4:10)
8. He grabbed him by the _____hand. (3:7)

SR

Art: Corbin Hillam

The words of an uneducated man —

The Council realized that Peter and John were both illiterate Galileans, but were amazed at how smart they sounded. Find out what Peter said by solving the code below.

Put the letter that immediately follows each letter alphabetically in the blank. (Z = A)

KDS HS AD JMNVM SN ZKK NE XNT, ZMC SN ZKK SGD ODNOKD NE HRQZDK, SGZS SGHR LZM HR RSZMCHMF ADENQD XNT HM FNNC GDZKSG AX SGD MZLD NE IDRTR BGQHRS NE MZYZQDSG, VGNL XNT BQTBHEHDC, VGNL FNC QZHRDC EQNL SGD CDZC.

— *Check your answer by looking up* Acts 4:10.

SR
Art: Terry Sirrell

Journal Lesson 10

When are you called to speak out boldly?

SR

Art: Terry Sirrell

PENTECOST

REPORTER: Hello. This is Ruth, your reporter on the street. We are here in Jerusalem, observing the people from many different lands who have gathered here for the Pentecost festival. The disciples of Jesus are here too. These disciples believe that Jesus is the Son of God. Just a minute, folks. There seems to be some disturbance.

(sounds of violent wind)

REPORTER: This is so odd, but with that rush of wind you just heard there are flames—tongues of fire—and they are resting over the heads of the disciples of Jesus. The crowd is gathering around them.

(crowd noises)

REPORTER: The disciples are speaking in many languages and the crowd is listening. Now one man is speaking. I believe his name is Peter. Let's listen in . . .

PETER: For the promise is for you, for your children, and for all who are far away . . .

REPORTER: Let me call one of the visitors of Jerusalem over here. Sir, can you tell me what is happening?

VISITOR: I just heard in my own language the amazing story of Jesus. When I get home, I will tell everyone what I have learned.

REPORTER: Thank you, sir. Now let me see if I can speak to one of the disciples. Are you a disciple of Jesus?

DISCIPLE: Yes, I am; and Jesus promised he would send us a helper. That's what happened today. We have been filled with the Holy Spirit and given the ability to speak in languages we do not know. We were able to tell these visitors about Jesus.

REPORTER: Thank you. Well folks, this has been an amazing Pentecost festival. People from many lands have heard the story of Jesus. They will go back home and tell others what they have heard.

THANKS TO THE COMING OF THE HOLY SPIRIT TODAY AT PENTECOST, MANY PEOPLE WILL LEARN ABOUT JESUS AND THE CHRISTIAN FAITH.

Pentecost Fans

FOLD

NR BR SR

Art: F. S. Davis

Color the Picture

NR

Art: Charles Jakubowski

HIDDEN PENTECOST MESSAGE

Spring 2005, Lesson 11

BR

Art: Bob Jones

75

CHRISTIANS AROUND THE WORLD

At Pentecost, the disciples were given the ability to speak in languages they did not know. Now there are Christians all over the world who speak many different languages. Practice saying "We are Christians" in the languages below.

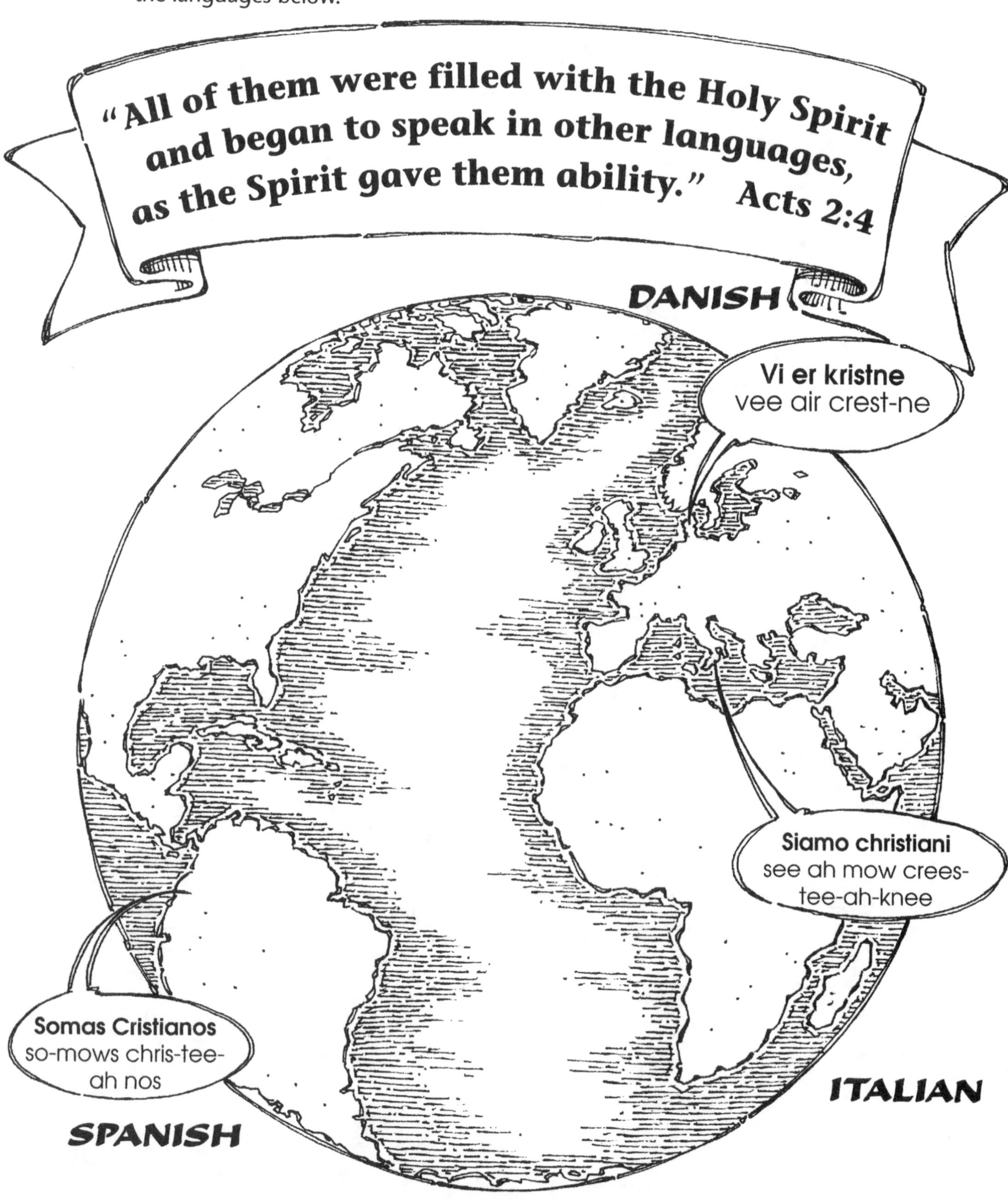

BR SR

Art: Robbie Short

BIBLE MONEY

In New Testament times, coins were confusing!

There were Roman coins, Greek coins, and Jewish coins—each that were worth different amounts of money. Use the information below and place each coin name in the correct column and in the correct order from the smallest coin to the largest coin.

Hint: Think of a Roman "as" like a quarter in today's money.

1. A Jewish *lepton, or mite,* was worth half a Roman *quadron.*

2. A Greek *mina* was worth 100 Greek *drachmas.*

3. One Roman *denarius* was worth about 16 Roman *as.*

4. One Roman *as* was worth about one-quarter of one Roman *quadron.*

5. A Greek *drachma* was worth about the same as a Roman *denarius.*

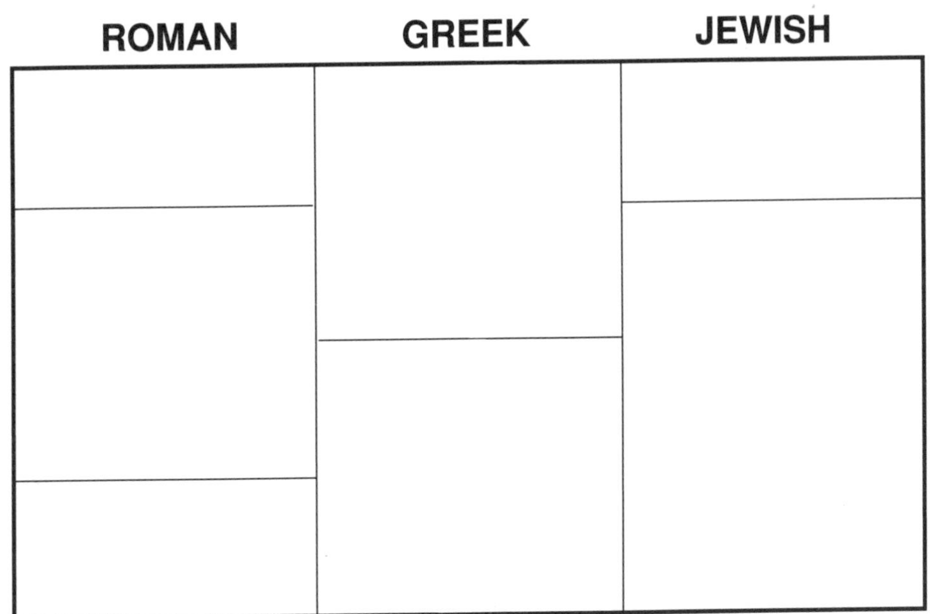

ROMAN	GREEK	JEWISH

Art: Yoshi Miyake

Journal Lesson 11

All of them were filled with the Holy Spirit.

Seven Chosen to Serve

NARRATOR: Now as word got out, more and more people became followers of Jesus. And as the number of followers grew, there became more and more problems.

NEWCOMERS: We are hungry. We are poor. You are neglecting us.

DISCIPLES: We are teachers. We are preachers. Our job is to pray for the good of all.

NARRATOR: All the people came together. They gave their belongings to the group so that the food and clothing could be distributed to everyone. Followers of Jesus should help one another.

NEWCOMERS: We are hungry. We are poor. You are neglecting us.

DISCIPLES: We are teachers. We are preachers. Our job is to pray for the good of all.

NARRATOR: Soon it became a matter of what was more important.

NEWCOMERS: We are hungry. We are poor. You are neglecting us.

DISCIPLES: We are teachers. We are preachers. Our job is to pray for the good of all.

NARRATOR: What was the solution? Everyone had needs. Everyone had issues.

NEWCOMERS: We are hungry. We are poor. You are neglecting us.

DISCIPLES: We are teachers. We are preachers. Our job is to pray for the good of all.

NARRATOR: So the disciples came up with this solution. They needed helpers. Then the disciples could preach and teach and pray. The helpers would help the poor and feed the hungry and care for the needs of all.

The people chose seven from the community to be the helpers. And everyone was happy. No one was neglected. And the Word of God continued to spread.

Based on Acts 6:1-7
Written by Lee Dell Stickler

I Am a Helper

Write your name on the job chart. Ask your family to help you decide jobs for you to do this week. Make a check mark each time you do a job.

Name: ______________________________

Job 1. ______________________________

2. ______________________________

3. ______________________________

Monday			
Tuesday			
Wednesday			
Thursday			
Friday			

BR SR
Art: Brenda Gilliam

What do followers of Jesus do?

Find the words in the puzzle that tell what followers of Jesus do today.

worship	pray
serve	share
praise	work
care	love
help	give

K	G	I	V	E	P	H
B	F	S	C	A	R	E
H	L	E	D	S	A	L
W	O	R	S	H	I	P
O	V	V	G	A	S	R
R	E	E	I	R	E	A
K	C	E	J	E	A	Y

Art: Yoshi Miyake

Use Your Bible

Read Acts 2:43-47 to find the missing words.
Then fill in the "People Puzzles."

Awe came upon everyone, because many wonders and ___(6)___were being done by the apostles. All who believed were together and had all things in common; they __(1)__ their possessions and __(3)___ and distribute the ___(7)___ to all, as any had need. Day by day, as they ___(9)___ much ___(8)___together in the Temple, they ___(4)___ ___(5)___at home and ate their food with glad and generous hearts, ___(2)___God and having the goodwill of all the people. And day by day the Lord added to their numbers those who were being ___(10)____. Acts 2:43-47

Art: Corbin Hillam

The disciples chose helpers. Color the picture.

Art: David Schimmell

Journal Lesson 12

Who are the leaders in my church?

How can I serve in the church?

How can I serve as a disciple in the world?

Jobs in the Church

Most likely your church has some people who are paid to do some of the work. But sometimes the church needs help. Talk to one of the leaders in your church and see which jobs in your church are done by paid employees and which are done by volunteers.

	Paid Employees	Volunteers
CLEANING THE SANCTUARY AFTER WORSHIP		
COOKING FOR CHURCH MEALS		
TEACHING SUNDAY SCHOOL		
TAKING CARE OF BABIES IN THE NURSERY		
VISITING SICK PEOPLE IN THE HOSPITAL		
GREETING WORSHIPERS AS THEY ARRIVE		
PRINTING AND FOLDING THE WORSHIP BULLETIN		
MOWING THE GRASS AROUND THE CHURCH		
OTHER JOBS		

Which of the above jobs could you do?

Art: Corbin Hillam

A Letter From Dorcas
To my friend in the churches:

Greetings!

I am Dorcas. You may have heard of me. My friend, Luke, heard my story and took some notes for a book he said he was working on.

If you have heard of me, you probably know how Peter brought me back from death. I don't remember much about it to tell you the truth. All I know is that I got really sick and that people started hanging around my bedside whispering in hushed tones. The next thing I remember is opening my eyes. There was Peter staring me in the face. Anyway, talk about a second chance at life!

As spectacular as that day was for me, the real reason I'm writing is to tell you why I am a Christian and how it has changed me. Some people came to my synagogue one day telling amazing stories about a man named Jesus from Nazareth. They said that he was the Messiah and that trust in him brought God's salvation. I saw them heal people right before my eyes. They even said that I could be baptized and receive the power of Jesus' Spirit to share in the ministry he began. So I was baptized and began to worship with a group of Christians. For the first time, I felt like a whole person. The Christians valued my opinions; they celebrated the things I did well. They helped me see how a woman could use her life to serve others the way Jesus served. I began to care for the poorest people in our community. I especially enjoyed using my weaving skills to make clothes for the widows who had no families to support them.

So I am twice blessed by God. Not only did I get another chance at living, but I also found new life sharing in Jesus' ministry. You should do so as well!

Your friend,
Dorcas

(Based on Acts 9:36-42)
Story by Fred Edie.

Helper's Mitt

SUPPLIES: flannel or other soft cloth, leather punch, lacing (plastic or leather—available in craft stores), felt, glue, scissors, yarn

PREPARATION: Cut two mitt patterns from flannel for each child. Using the leather punch make holes one inch apart around the edge of the mitt (cut so that holes match up between patterns for "sewing"). Also, cut two eyes from felt and a 2" piece of yarn for the mouth.

OPTION: Glue mitt patterns together instead of sewing.

INSTRUCTIONS FOR THE CHILDREN:

1. "Sew" the mitts together with the lacing. Tie off the lacing at both ends.
2. Glue the eyes and mouth onto the mitt.
3. Practice dusting with the mitt. The mitt works best if you wear the face on the back side of your hand.
4. Take your mitt home and ask what you can dust!

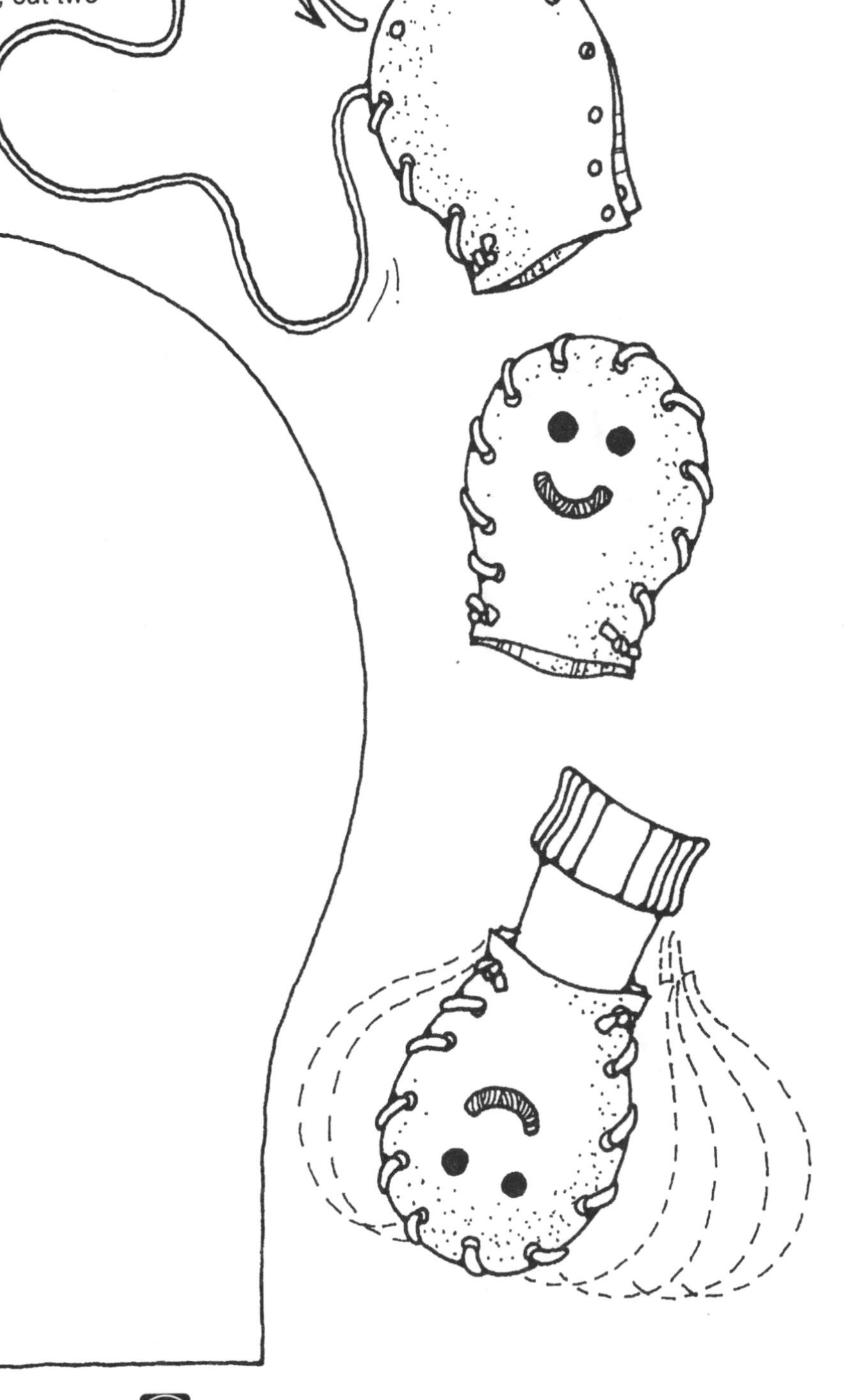

Art: Brenda Gilliam

Color the Picture

NR

Art: Benton Mahan

RECOGNIZING MY GIFTS

Each of us has gifts that make us special. Put a check next to the picture that shows a gift you have. Draw a picture of your special gift in the box at right.

What's in a Name?

Luke tells us of a woman whose name in Aramaic (ar-uh-MA-ik) was Tabitha, which is usually translated to the Greek, Dorcas. Aramean (ar-uh-Me-uhn) was the language most of the Jews spoke at the time of Jesus, but Greek was the official language of the Roman empire. So, Tabitha/Dorcas had two names. There are other people in the Bible who had two names. Use the crossword clues below to find the names of these people.

ACROSS

1. Also known as 7 across (Genesis 32:28)
3. Also known as 6 across (Acts 13:9)
5. Also known as 3 down (Matthew 16:17-18)
6. Also known as 3 across (Acts 13:9)
7. Also known as 1 across (Genesis 32:28)
9. Also known as 8 down (Genesis 17:15)

DOWN:

2. Also known as 4 down (Daniel 1:7)
3. Also known as 5 across (Matthew 16:17-18)
4. Also known as 2 down (Daniel 1:7)
8. Also known as 9 across (Genesis 17:15)

Art: Corbin Hillam

How could Jared, Maggie, and Montez help their friends to show that they care?

JARED: Hey Thomas, what's up? You weren't at baseball practice today.

THOMAS: Yeah, well, I'm not going out for the team this year.

JARED: No way! Hey, man, we need you. You're the best player on the team.

THOMAS: Sorry, but I don't have any cleats and my glove is shot. There is no way I can ask my folks for more stuff. We're stretched pretty tight as it is.

MAGGIE: Lucy, are you OK? You are definitely not yourself.

LUCY: Well, I haven't really said anything, but my mom told me last night that my Gramma's cancer is back and this time it's worse.

MAGGIE: Bummer!

LUCY: Yeah, and while she goes back in the hospital, my mom is going to have to spend a lot of time there, which means I'm on my own after school to get my own dinner, watch TV by myself, and put myself to bed. Oh, shoot, that sounds so selfish. My Gramma is going to die, and I'm complaining about being alone.

MONTEZ: Whoa! What happened to you?

ERIC: Oh, I was being stupid and trying to show off. I fell trying this new skateboarding trick. And now I have a broken leg and will have to be on crutches for at least the next three weeks. It's going to be so awful. I can put my books in my backpack, but what about the cafeteria line? And my locker is on the bottom row. I don't know how I'm going to bend over to get into it. And then there's the problem of my baritone. I guess I won't get to take it home to practice. I can't believe I was so stupid!

Art: Terry Sirrell

Journal for Lesson 13

Write or draw about the gifts God has given you that you can share with others.

SR
Art: Corbin Hillam